Harwood Fundamentals of Pure and Applied Economics

UNCERTAINTY AND THE THEORY OF INTERNATIONAL TRADE

Routledge
Taylor & Francis Group
LONDON AND NEW YORK

FUNDAMENTALS OF PURE AND APPLIED ECONOMICS

EDITORS IN CHIEF

J. LESOURNE, Conservatoire National des Arts et Métiers, Paris, France

H. SONNENSCHEIN, University of Pennsylvania, Philadelphia, PA, USA

ADVISORY BOARD

K. ARROW, Stanford, CA, USA
W. BAUMOL, Princeton, NJ, USA
W. A. LEWIS, Princeton, NJ, USA
S. TSURU, Tokyo, Japan

INTERNATIONAL ECONOMICS I
In 3 Volumes

I	Game Theory in International Economics	*Mcmillan*
II	Uncertainty and the Theory of International Trade	*Grinols*
III	Disequilibrium Trade Theories	*Itoh and Negishi*

UNCERTAINTY AND THE THEORY OF INTERNATIONAL TRADE

EARL L GRINOLS

LONDON AND NEW YORK

First published in 1987 by
Harwood Academic Publishers GmbH

Published in 2001 by
Routledge
2 Park Square, Milton Park, Abingdon, Oxfordshire OX14 4RN
711 Third Avenue, New York, NY 10017

First issued in paperback 2014

Routledge is an imprint of the Taylor & Francis Group, an informa company

© 1987 Harwood Academic Publishers GmbH

All rights reserved. No part of this book may be reprinted or reproduced
or utilized in any form or by any electronic, mechanical,
or other means, now known or hereafter invented, including photocopying
and recording, or in any information storage or retrieval system, without
permission in writing from the publishers.

The publishers have made every effort to contact authors/copyright holders
of the works reprinted in *Harwood Fundamentals of Pure & Applied Economics*.
This has not been possible in every case, however, and we would welcome
correspondence from those individuals/companies we have been unable to
trace.

These reprints are taken from original copies of each book. in many cases
the condition of these originals is not perfect. the publisher has gone to
great lengths to ensure the quality of these reprints, but wishes to point
out that certain characteristics of the original copies will, of necessity, be
apparent in reprints thereof.

British Library Cataloguing in Publication Data
A CIP catalogue record for this book
is available from the British Library

Uncertainty and the Theory of International Trade

International Economics I: 3 Volumes

Harwood Fundamentals of Pure & Applied Economics

ISBN: 978-0-415-26910-0 (hbk)
ISBN: 978-0-415-75362-3 (pbk)

Uncertainty and the Theory of International Trade

Earl L. Grinols
University of Illinois, USA

A volume in the International Trade section
edited by
Murray Kemp
University of New South Wales, Australia

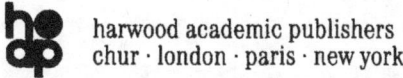

harwood academic publishers
chur · london · paris · new york

© 1987 by Harwood Academic Publishers GmbH
Poststrasse 22, 7000 Chur, Switzerland
All rights reserved

Harwood Academic Publishers

Post Office Box 197
London WC2E 9PX
England

58, rue Lhomond
75005 Paris
France

Post Office Box 786
Cooper Station
New York, NY 10276
United States of America

Library of Congress Cataloging-in-Publication Data

Grinols, Earl L., 1951–
  Uncertainty and the theory of international trade.

  (Fundamentals of pure and applied economics,
vol. 15. International trade section, ISSN 0191-1708)
  Bibliography: p.
  Includes index.
  1. Commercial policy. 2. Rational expectations
(Economic theory) 3. Commerce. I. Title. II. Series:
Fundamentals of pure and applied economics; vol. 15.
III. Series: Fundamentals of pure and applied
economics. International trade section.
HF1411.G72   1986   382.1'04   86-19566
ISBN 3-7186-0356-X

No part of this book may be reproduced or utilized in any form or
by any means, electronic or mechanical, including photocopying and
recording, or by any information storage or retrieval system, without
permission in writing from the publishers.

Contents

Introduction to the Series	vii
Introduction: Risk and Trade	1
1. Basic Concepts	4
2. Uncertainty and Security Markets: Demand	9
3. Uncertainty and Production: Supply	16
4. The Theorems of International Trade Theory	27
5. The Gains from Trade	50
6. Tariffs and Quotas	61
7. Commercial Policy	77
Appendix	88
References	89
Index	93

Introduction to the Series

Drawing on a personal network, an economist can still relatively easily stay well informed in the narrow field in which he works, but to keep up with the development of economics as a whole is a much more formidable challenge. Economists are confronted with difficulties associated with the rapid development of their discipline. There is a risk of "balkanisation" in economics, which may not be favorable to its development.

Fundamentals of Pure and Applied Economics has been created to meet this problem. The discipline of economics has been subdivided into sections (listed inside). These sections include short books, each surveying the state of the art in a given area.

Each book starts with the basic elements and goes as far as the most advanced results. Each should be useful to professors needing material for lectures, to graduate students looking for a global view of a particular subject, to professional economists wishing to keep up with the development of their science, and to researchers seeking convenient information on questions that incidentally appear in their work.

Each book is thus a presentation of the state of the art in a particular field rather than a step-by-step analysis of the development of the literature. Each is a high-level presentation but accessible to anyone with a solid background in economics, whether engaged in business, government, international organizations, teaching, or research in related fields.

Three aspects of *Fundamentals of Pure and Applied Economics* should be emphasized:

—First, the project covers the whole field of economics, not only theoretical or mathematical economics.

—Second, the project is open-ended and the number of books is not predetermined. If new interesting areas appear, they will generate additional books.

—Last, all the books making up each section will later be grouped to constitute one or several volumes of an Encyclopedia of Economics.

The editors of the sections are outstanding economists who have selected as authors for the series some of the finest specialists in the world.

J. Lesourne   *H. Sonnenschein*

Uncertainty and the Theory of International Trade

EARL L. GRINOLS†

University of Illinois, Urbana, USA

RISK AND TRADE

The study of uncertainty and the theory of international trade has adapted in the dozen or so years of its existence to an understanding of the need for explicitly modeling risk sharing and trade in risk as distinct from trade in commodities. Commodity trade theory has usually been conducted from the point of view of the trading nation. The introduction of risk necessarily changes this emphasis for the reason that a single individual or a nation of identical representative individuals cannot trade internally in risk. The traditional tool of assuming that a benevolent central authority re-distributes income domestically according to a social welfare function (causing the nation to behave in world trade as if it is maximizing a one-consumer utility function) is also inappropriate. The use of lump sum transfers implies that the central authroity through its transfers is implicitly providing risk-sharing services. Unless the planner is limited in some way in the transfers he can make, or private markets internally are perfect in providing risk sharing opportunities, the use of the national perspective without reference to individual households who differ from one another is a misleading representation of reality.

Faced with this circumstance, this monograph brings together several strands, including information from the pure finance literature and industrial organization literature on firm behavior in response to risk, to present a unified treatment of uncertainty and international trade theory.

The topics which are included are organized around the risk-

---

† I would like to thank Murray Kemp for initiating this project.

sharing opportunities of the individual, and in particular, the types of securities which are available for sharing risk. After describing the Arrow–Debreu general equilibrium framework in Chapter 1, the first topic considered in the following chapter is a simple model of portfolio choice for the individual. The individual's ultimate concern is the consumption of goods and services in future states of nature, but he responds to changes in risk by adjusting his ownership of risky securities as well as directly altering consumptions. His welfare is therefore dependent on commodity trading opportunities (international trade) as well as the set of securities for trading risk.

But consumption is only one-half of international trade. To understand trade, which is the difference between consumption and production, one must provide a theory of production. Here, the firm's ultimate objective is to generate profits in future states of nature. But just as the consumer's choices indirectly cause a demand for risky securities, so the firm's choices indirectly generate a supply of risky securities. In both demand and supply, equilibrium consequently depends a great deal on how many, and what type of risky securities are available for trade in the markets. Chapter 3 accordingly delves into the theory of the firm under uncertainty, providing a generalization which goes somewhat beyond the conventional models currently employed. Chapters 2 and 3 describe how the popular special cases involving trade with complete security markets, incomplete security markets, and no security markets can be analyzed as parts of the common framework. International trade in securities and the special assumption of multiplicative production uncertainty are also treated.

The rest of the monograph addresses the comparative statics and welfare properties of trade under uncertainty. The choice of topics is determined by the desire to provide a treatment which will parallel the main body of deterministic trade theory. The majority of the theory is presented in the context of a workable two good-two factor extension of the Heckscher–Ohlin framework, except in cases where a full general equilibrium construction provides a more general result with less effort. The reader familiar with the core of trade theory as represented in the 2×2 general equilibrium model should have no trouble recognizing the layout of Chapters 4 through 7.

Chapter 4 re-examines of the major theorems of international trade theory: The Stolper–Samuelson, Rybczynski, Heckscher–Ohlin, and Factor Price Equalization theorems and the price-output relation. All of the theorems need not hold under uncertainty. Different responses of the model depend on the nature of the markets for risk, whether production risk is in the set spanned by traded securities and so on. A number of new results are proved which serve to tie together the existing literature. Chapter 5 considers the gains from trade under uncertainty. Several results available in the literature are generalized, and a framework for analysis is provided which explains why traditional proofs of gains from trade which apply in a deterministic model do not necessarily carry over to conditions of risk. Chapters 6 and 7 form a unit in that both deal with commerical policy under uncertainty. Chapter 6 discusses tariffs and quotas separately in view of their special importance. Chapter 7 then provides a general format within which the welfare effects of any commerical policy can be broken down into monopoly price effects in commodity markets, monopoly price effects in risk markets, improved risk-sharing effects, distribution of ownership income effects and standard effects from deterministic welfare policy.

Throughout the writing of this monograph the overriding consideration has been that it should present a unified and readable, but not overly technical, treatment of the subject matter from a well defined point of view or perspective. This approach necessarily requires a choice of which material should be emphasized and which de-emphasized. I have chosen here to organize around the principle of the degee of risk-sharing available to the consumer through markets in claims to firm output. References to what I think are a minimal set of readings for an understanding of the field are given in bibliographic notes at the end of the chapters. This choice was taken partly because of the presence of several recent and very good literature surveys which the reader may consider complementary to the treatment here.

Bibliographic Notes

The field has been covered in depth at various times in several monographs and surveys. The reader is directed to Batra [1975],

Helpman and Razin [1978] and Pomery [1979]. An excellent up-to-date survey of the literature is available in Pomery [1984].

1. BASIC CONCEPTS

This chapter introduces the basic framework for discussing uncertainty and the theory of international trade. Three things are done. The elements of the model are presented, uncertainty is introduced, and the Heckscher–Ohlin-like production framework is given for the uncertain environment.

A. Elements of the economy

We will discuss the theory of international trade and uncertainty within the context of a Debreu-type economy as described, for example, in *Theory of Value* or in Arrow and Hahn, *General Competitive Analysis*. This framework is broad enough to incorporate virtually every major question of interest with the exception of questions requiring an infinite time horizon.

The following notation will be followed. Given a positive integer l, let R^l denote l-dimensional Euclidean space; and R^l_+ the nonnegative orthant of R^l. If x and y are vectors in R^l, let $x \cdot y$ denote the inner product of x and y, $\sum_h x_h y_h$, where x_h and y_h represent the hth components of x and y, respectively.

The model of the world economy with l commodities, m consumers and n firms can now be reviewed. From the point of view of the world a commodity bundle is a point x in R^l where x_h describes the quantity of commodity h. Commodities are distinguished by their type, location, date of delivery, and, in the case of uncertainty, by state of nature of delivery. Different commodities generally will have different market prices. Hence, an umbrella scheduled for delivery tomorrow if it rains will typically sell for a different contract price than the same umbrella scheduled for delivery tomorrow if it does not rain.

Producers are numbered $j = 1, \ldots, n$. The output of producer j is a vector $y_j \in R^l$ whose positive components represent net output levels and whose negative components represent net input levels or use of factors. For each firm, output y_j must be chosen from the production set, Y_j, a set of feasible productions $Y_j \subset R^l$. With market prices for commodities given by $p \in R^l$, the market value of firm j is equal to the present value of its profit earned, $p \cdot y_j$. If there is only one period and no uncertainty, this is the standard measure of current profit.

In the two industry case $y_1(\alpha) - F_1(K_1, L_1, \alpha) \le 0$ and $y_2(\alpha) - F_2(K_2, L_2, \alpha) \le 0$ are the production sets of industries 1 and 2 where $y_j(\alpha)$ is output of good j in state of nature α and $F_j(\cdot)$ are production functions dependent on the state of nature α and factor inputs K_j and L_j.[1] Let $p_j(\alpha)$ represent the spot prices for good j in state of nature α, and let w and r be the wage rate for labor and the rental rate of capital, respectively. Deterministic values for w and r result in the case where factor services are contracted for at the beginning of the production period for the certain remunerations w, r. The future state-dependent profit of firm j is then,

$$\pi_j(\alpha) \equiv p_j(\alpha) F_j(K_j, L_j, \alpha) - \rho w L_j - \rho r K_j,$$

where ρ represents the one period riskless interest rate.

Consumers are represented by their preference ordering $\succcurlyeq_i \subset R^l \times R^l$, and consumption set $X_i \subset R^l$. The preference ordering is interpreted in the following way. If $x \in X_i$, $P \subset R^l$ then $(x, P) \in \succcurlyeq_i$ indicates that all points x' in set P are preferred or indifferent to x. This is summarized by writing $x' \succcurlyeq_i x$. We assume that $\succcurlyeq_i$ is *complete* and *transitive* meaning that all x, x', x'' in R^l can be ranked by $\succcurlyeq_i$ relative to one another, and that $x'' \succcurlyeq_i x'$, $x' \succcurlyeq_i x$ implies $x'' \succcurlyeq_i x$.

A country k consists of a set of producers (Y_j), consumers $(X_i, \succcurlyeq_i)$ and initial endowment of goods $\omega_k \in R^l$, where the set of consumers i and producers j are a subset of world consumers $i = 1, \ldots, m$ and $j = 1, \ldots, n$, respectively. Let $i, j \in C_k$ refer to those i and j making up country k.

A world allocation is a set of consumptions and production

---

[1] That is, production in industries 1 and 2 is given by,

$$y_1 = (y_1(1), \ldots, y_1(\alpha), \ldots, y_1(S); 0, \ldots, 0; -K_1, -L_1) \in R^{2S+2}$$
$$y_2 = (0, \ldots, 0; y_2(1), \ldots, y_2(\alpha), \ldots, y_2(S); -K_2, -L_2) \in R^{2S+2}$$

where the commodities consist of output of the two goods in each state of nature $\alpha = 1, \ldots, S$, and capital and labor services in production.

choices $((x^i), (y_j))$, $x^i, y_j \in R^l$. The trade vector of country k is equal to $z_k \in R^l$ where $\sum_{i \in C_k} x^i - \sum_{j \in C_k} y_j - \omega_k \equiv z_k$. A world allocation is feasible if $x^i \in X_i$, $y_j \in Y_j$ for all i and j, and $\sum_k z_k = 0$.

B. Uncertainty

Examination of the physical components of the world economy $((X_i, \succcurlyeq_i), (Y_j), \omega_k)$ reveals that the exogenous uncertainty enters the system through its effect on production, endowments, and preferences. For example, the production functions $F_j(K_j, L_j, \alpha)$ involve the random state of nature α, and endowments ω_k depend on the state of nature. Uncertainty also affects the structure of consumption sets X_i and preferences $\succcurlyeq_i$ since goods are distinguished by the state of nature. For example, the list of alternative subsistence bundles in X_i may differ when α is restricted to one state of nature rather than another.[2] Rankings between commodities will also typically depend upon which state of nature is being considered.

Because of the dependence of the economy on exogenous uncertainty, endogenous prices will also typically depend upon which state of nature occurs. An individual firm or household will therefore typically face price uncertainty as well as uncertainty originating in production and consumption sets.

C. The non-deterministic model of production

The basic Heckscher–Ohlin model of international trade as developed by Samuelson and others is a versatile and elegant tool for studying in an open economy the general equilibrium cross relationship between prices and quantities, prices and prices, and quantities and quantities in factor and output markets. This flexibility in the model requires at least two factors, two goods and two countries. Extensions of the basic properties discovered in this setting can then

---

[2] As a simple example, let the two states of nature be "warm" and "cold." The four commodities are "food" and "clothing" in each of the two states with minimal consumption being 1 unit of food regardless of the state of nature, and 1 unit of clothing if it is warm. If the state is "cold," however, 2 units of clothing are needed. The consumption set if the state is "warm" consists of food and clothing bundles with greater than 1 unit of each. If it is "cold," two units or more of clothing are needed.

be carried out in terms of multiple factors and multiple goods. The extension discussed here is the introduction of uncertainty.

In the determinsitic model marketclearing decisions are made simultaneously in equilibrium. The presence of uncertainty, however, requires a description of the sequencing of decisions with respect to uncertainty and, hence, some recognition of the role of time. In the complete markets formulation of uncertainty and trade (exemplified, for example in Dumas [1980] or in section 4 of Chang, Ethier and Kemp [1980]) production decisions are made before the resolution of uncertainty and factors are paid at certain rates which are contracted for at the beginning of the period. Consumers' portfolio decisions are similarly made before the resolution of uncertainty. Consumption is chosen from the proceeds of their investments after the state of nature is revealed. Thus factors are assigned to production at the start of the period and consumers make portfolio choices at the same time. The state of nature is then revealed and consumers consume out of their earnings as owners of factors and portfolio capital. The nature of the production uncertainty and the extent of markets for portfolio risk determine the effect of uncertainty on the model.

Production. The commodities y_1 and y_2 are produced by two factors capital K and labor L according to the production relations,

$$y_1(\alpha) = F_1(K_1, L_1, \alpha) \tag{1.1}$$

$$y_2(\alpha) = F_2(K_2, L_2, \alpha). \tag{1.2}$$

F_1 and F_2 are linearly homogeneous of degree 1 in capital and labor, and twice continuously differentiable. First derivatives in K and L are positive, second derivatives are negative, and second cross derivatives are non-negative.

Firms contract for the services of capital and labor at the start of the period. Payments are made at the end of the period in the amounts $w\rho$ and $r\rho$ per unit of service where ρ is one plus the one-period rate of interest.[3]

Let an elementary security $e_\alpha = (0, \ldots, 1, \ldots, 0) \in R^S$ be an

---

[3] Equivalently, payments could be made at the start of the period in the amounts w and r.

asset paying one unit of numeraire if state of nature α occurs and zero otherwise. Assume that e_α, $\alpha = 1, \ldots, S$, are traded on security markets and have prices $\beta(\alpha)$. Writing the end-of-period price of commodity j in state α as $p_j(\alpha)$, the end-of-period profits of firms 1 and 2 are given by,

$$\pi_1(\alpha) = p_1(\alpha)F_1(K_1, L_1, \alpha) - w\rho L_1 - r\rho K_1 \quad (1.3)$$

$$\pi_2(\alpha) = p_2(\alpha)F_2(K_2, L_2, \alpha) = w\rho L_2 - r\rho K_2. \quad (1.4)$$

Since the firm's profits across states α are equivalent to the payment of $\pi_j(\alpha)$ units of securities e_α their value must be the sum $\sum_\alpha \beta(\alpha)\pi_j(\alpha) = P_j - wL_j - rK_j$ where P_j is the market value of the firm's random output. The firm's problem is,

$$\underset{\{K_j, L_j\}}{\text{Maximize}}\; P_j - wL_j - rK_j \quad (1.5)$$

which implies that,[4]

$$\sum_\alpha \beta(\alpha)p_1(\alpha)\frac{\partial F_1}{\partial K_1} - r \le 0 \quad (1.6)$$

$$\sum_\alpha \beta(\alpha)p_1(\alpha)\frac{\partial F_1}{\partial L_1} - w \le 0 \quad (1.7)$$

$$\sum_\alpha \beta(\alpha)p_2(\alpha)\frac{\partial F_2}{\partial K_2} - r \le 0 \quad (1.8)$$

$$\sum_\alpha \beta(\alpha)p_2(\alpha)\frac{\partial F_2}{\partial L_2} - w \le 0. \quad (1.9)$$

Demand for factor services is determined by (1.6)–(1.9) where strict inequality in (1.6) implies $K_1 = 0$ and similarly for (1.7), (1.8), (1.9) with respect to L_1, K_2, L_2. Supply of factors is given by $\sum_i K^i = K$ $\sum_i L^i = L$ where (K^i, L^i) is the endowment of consumer i of factor services in capital and labor. Marketclearing in factors is therefore given by

$$K_1 + K_2 = K \quad (1.10)$$

$$L_1 + L_2 = L. \quad (1.11)$$

---

[4] The simplification $\sum_\alpha \beta(\alpha)\rho = 1$ follows because one unit of numeraire invested at the rate ρ pays ρ units in each future state. Such an asset must have present value of 1.

Given prices $\beta(\alpha), p_1(\alpha)$, and $p_2(\alpha)$ equations (1.1)–(1.11) determine the assignment of capital and labor to production, factor rewards, the value of firm output, and the quantities of goods y_1 and y_2 in each state of nature.

D. Summary

Uncertainty enters the economic system through the state dependence of endowments, production, and consumption sets. Goods are also characterized by their state of nature of delivery. In this chapter the basic Heckscher–Ohlin production framework was extended to uncertainty.

E. Bibliographic notes

For general equilibrium treatments of uncertainty see Debreu [1959], Arrow and Hahn [1971]. The model of this section is treated in Dumas [1980] and Chang, Ethier and Kemp [1980], especially Section 4. Other references to variations on the basic model will be given at specific points later.

2. UNCERTAINTY AND SECURITY MARKETS: DEMAND

Much of international trade theory examines the general equilibrium structure of production and the effect of changing prices on output, real factor rewards, production techniques, and so on. In this chapter we discuss the effects of uncertainty on the demand side of the model. When uncertainty is introduced into trade, the constellation of relevant prices is enlarged to include prices for risk $\beta(\alpha)$ and spot prices for commodities in different states of nature $p_j(\alpha)$. Prices in the risk markets are formed through the interactions between the portfolio decisions of consumers and production decisions of firms. The consumption decisions of consumers and the supply of commodities determine spot prices for output. It is therefore necessary to distinguish between the individual as investor and the individual as consumer. In the following section some results based on the simplest possible model are presented.

A. The individual as investor: choosing his portfolio

In this section assume that the preferences of the individual can be represented by a utility function of the form:

$$U^i = W^i(x^i; s) \qquad (2.1')$$

where x^i is the vector $x^i = (x_1^i(1), x_2^i(1); \ldots ; x_1^i(\alpha), x_2^i(\alpha); \ldots ; x_1^i(S), x_2^i(S))$ consisting of the individual's consumption of goods 1 and 2 in each future state of nature and s is the vector $(1, \ldots, S)$. For example, if the consumer's welfare rises with expected utility, $W^i(x^i)$ might take the expected utility form,

$$W^i(x^i) = \sum_\alpha \pi_\alpha^i V^i(x_1^i(\alpha), x_2^i(\alpha), \alpha) \qquad (2.1'')$$

where π_α^i is i's subjective probability that state α will occur, and V^i is i's elementary utility function for goods in state α. Since the state of nature is exogenous to the system, we have suppressed s in the notation of (2.1''). Once state α has been revealed, consumption of goods 1 and 2 must satisfy the individual's budget constraint,

$$p_1(\alpha)x_1^i(\alpha) + p_2(\alpha)x_2^i(\alpha) = I^i(\alpha) \qquad (2.2)$$

where $I^i(\alpha)$ is the available income in state of nature α. Letting $I^i = (I^i(1), \ldots, I^i(S))$ and $p = [\ldots, p_1(\alpha), p_2(\alpha), \ldots]$ the dependence of x^i on (I, p) is used to write utility in the indirect form,

$$U^i = U^i(I; p) \qquad (2.1)$$

which will be the form we will use to discuss the consumer's portfolio decisions.

As an investor, each individual is endowed with ownership of physical capital K^i, labor L^i, future goods $\omega_j^i(\alpha)$, and ownership shares in firms $\bar{\theta}_j^i$. Before α is known he purchases a portfolio of stock shares, borrowing or lending at the going rate of interest, subject to the wealth constraint,

$$\sum_j \bar{\theta}_j^i (P_j - wL_j - rK_j) = \sum_j \theta_j^i P_j + b^i \qquad (2.3)$$

where P_j is the market value of 100% ownership of firm j and b^i is the amount lent by the investor at market rate ρ. Once the portfolio is chosen, the income of i in state α is given by

$$I^i(\alpha) = \sum_j \theta^i_j p_j(\alpha) F_j(K_j, L_j, \alpha) + \rho r K^i + \rho w L^i$$
$$+ \rho b^i + \sum_j p_j(\alpha) \omega^i_j(\alpha). \qquad (2.4)$$

The formal problem of the consumer, therefore, is to choose $((\theta^i_j), b^i)$ to maximize (2.1) subject to (2.3) and (2.4) with the Lagrangian,

$$\mathcal{L} = U^i(I; p) + \lambda \left[\sum_j (\bar{\theta}^i_j - \theta^i_j) P_j - \bar{\theta}^i_j(wL_j - rK_j) - b^i \right].$$

Necessary first order conditions for an optimum are,

$$\sum_\alpha \beta^i(\alpha) p_j(\alpha) F_j(K_j, L_j, \alpha) = P_j$$
$$\sum_\alpha \beta^i(\alpha) \rho = 1 \qquad (2.5)$$

where $\beta^i(\alpha) = \sum_\alpha (\partial U^i/\partial I^i(\alpha))/\sum_\alpha (\partial U^i/\partial I^i(\alpha))\rho$. The notational similarity between $\beta^i(\alpha)$ and the market prices for pure securities $\beta(\alpha)$ introduced earlier is not accidental. This relationship is explored next.

B. Risk markets and the formation of risk prices

The asset market improves welfare by facilitating the trading of risk. The portfolio choices of investors determine the demand for assets depending on their risk characteristics. The induced market prices for risk therefore have welfare consequences for investors as they trade risk of different types between themselves.

On the supply side the markets for risk also have welfare consequences through the effect that risk prices have on production and inducing greater supply of certain financial securities. We will take that up in Chapter 3. In this section we demonstrate the insurance function of risk markets by showing in a 2-agent setting that: (1) the risk-neutral investor acts as a seller of insurance to the risk-averse individual, (2) the market acts to equalize agents' subjective values for traded securities regardless of the agent's personal attitudes towards risk, and (3) the types of securities traded determine the extent of agreement between agents over the value of different production choices of firms.

Let the two states of nature be $\alpha = 1, 2$ with equal probability of occurrence 1/2 for each. There are two investors, each of whom is endowed with half ownership of an asset which pays 95 if state 1 occurs and 105 if state 2 occurs. Both investors maximize expected utility, but investor 1 is risk neutral with

$$U^1 = E(I_\alpha^1) = \tfrac{1}{2}(I_1^1 + I_2^1) \tag{2.6}$$

whereas investor 2 is risk averse with

$$U^2 = E(\ln(I_\alpha^2)) = \tfrac{1}{2}(\ln I_1^2 + \ln I_2^2). \tag{2.6'}$$

The available income to investor i in future state α is given by

$$I_\alpha^i = \begin{cases} \theta^i 95 + b^i \rho & \text{if } \alpha = 1, \\ \theta^i 105 + b^i \rho & \text{if } \alpha = 2. \end{cases} \tag{2.7}$$

The first order conditions (2.5) for this example are,

$$\frac{0.5}{\lambda^1} 95 + \frac{0.5}{\lambda^1} 105 = P$$

$$\frac{0.5}{\lambda^1} \rho + \frac{0.5}{\lambda^1} \rho = 1 \tag{2.8}$$

for investor 1 and,

$$\frac{0.5}{\lambda^2 I_1^2} 95 + \frac{0.5}{\lambda^2 I_2^2} 105 = P$$

$$\frac{0.5}{\lambda^2 I_1^2} \rho + \frac{0.5}{\lambda^2 I_2^2} \rho = 1 \tag{2.8'}$$

for individual 2 where P is the price of the risky asset. From (2.8) we see that the market price of the asset paying (95, 105) is $100/\rho$ where ρ is one plus the riskless interest rate on bonds. Multiplying the second equation in (2.8′) by P and subtracting from the first implies that,

$$\frac{5}{2\lambda^2}\left[\frac{1}{I_2^2} - \frac{1}{I_1^2}\right] = 0 \tag{2.9}$$

which can only be satisfied if $\theta^2 = 0$. Thus the risk averse investor chooses to hold none of the risky asset in equilibrium, selling his holdings to investor 1, and lending at the riskless rate ρ to earn a certain income in the next period of 50. Direct calculation shows that his welfare is higher with an income of 50 than with the income he had previously of 47.5 in state 1 and 52.5 in state 2.

The example reveals two other features. First, although no riskless asset existed initially (borrowing and lending were zero), investors were able to write such contracts and did. In the final equilibrium investor 2 owns $50/\rho$ units of bonds written by investor 1.[5] Were a riskless asset unable to be traded, investor 2 could not sell his risk to investor 1 in return for units of the riskless asset, as occurred in this example, and welfare would fall. Second, although investor 2 is risk averse and investor 1 is risk neutral, both value the two traded assets identically. That is, the market has caused equalization of their initially disparate views on the value of the risky asset and the riskless bond. Risk has been traded from the risk-averse investor to the risk-neutral investor at a market price determined by the trade in securities. Effectively, investor 1 has sold an insurance policy to investor 2 for the beginning-of-period price $5/2\rho$ which pays 5 if state of nature 1 occurs. The combination of his original holdings plus the insurance policy gives investor 2 the same income at the end of the period regardless of the state of nature.

C. Security valuation and spanning

From the investor's Lagrangian in part A, the change in utility of investor i who is given in incremental quantity of security s paying $s(\alpha)$ in state α is proportional to.

$$\sum_i (\partial U^i/\partial I^i(\alpha))s(\alpha) = dU$$

Scaling by λ^i to convert to present value terms gives $dU/\lambda^i = \beta^i \cdot s$ where $\beta^i = (\beta^i(1), \ldots, \beta^i(S))$.

Turning to the valuation of securities in the simple example,

---

[5] The equilibrium can be shown to satisfy $b^2 = 50/\rho$, $\theta^2 = 0$ for investor 2 and $b^1 = -50/\rho$, $\theta^2 = 1$ for investor 1.

rearrangement of (2.8) and (2.8′) to put them in vector notation:

$$\begin{pmatrix} 95 & 105 \\ 1 & 1 \end{pmatrix} \begin{pmatrix} \beta^i(1) \\ \beta^i(2) \end{pmatrix} = \begin{pmatrix} P \\ 1/\rho \end{pmatrix}, \qquad (2.8'')$$

reveals that

$$\begin{pmatrix} \beta^1(1) \\ \beta^1(2) \end{pmatrix} = \begin{pmatrix} \beta^2(1) \\ \beta^2(2) \end{pmatrix} = \frac{1}{10} \begin{pmatrix} 105/\rho - P \\ P - 95/\rho \end{pmatrix}. \qquad (2.9)$$

Hence the market has equalized prices for risk for any type of security. The reader can convince himself that if there were 3 or more states of nature, $\beta^1(\alpha)$ need not equal $\beta^2(\alpha)$ for all α, as in the 2-state example above, but that the values for any traded security would continue to agree across investors.

This feature will be important in our discussion of the effect of international trade in securities and the theory of international trade. It can be encapsulated by introducing the notion of spanning from linear algebra. Let s_j be a vector in R^S whose elements represent the payments to an investor holding security j. For example, in the 2-state example a security paying 1 if state 1 occurred and zero otherwise would be given by $s = e_1 = (1, 0)$. Then any vector which can be written as the sum $\sum_{j \in J} a_j s_j$ for scalars a_j is said to be *spanned* by the set $\{s_j\}_{j \in J}$. The following proposition emerges.

PROPOSITION 2.1 *Any security, whether traded or not, which is spanned by a set of traded securities will be valued identically by all investors.*

The proof can be indicated by referring to our example. Security e_1 is not directly traded. However it is equal to 105/10 units of the riskless asset (paying $(1, 1)$ at market price $1/\rho$) less 1/10 units of the risky asset (paying $(95, 105)$ at market price P) which has value $(105/10\rho - P/10)$ by (2.5) (or (2.9)) which is the same regardless of which investor is consulted. Arbitrage between identical products insures that the proposition applies.

In the special case where traded securities span the entire space of securities, all securities are valued identically by investors.

PROPOSITION 2.2 *If the set of traded securities spans R^S, any security, whether traded or not, will be valued identically by all investors.*

Let $\mathscr{S} \subset R^S$ be the set spanned by the set of traded securities $\{s_j\}$. It is easy to show that if $x, y \in \mathscr{S}$ then $aX \in \mathscr{S}$ for scalar a and also $x + y \in \mathscr{S}$. If we add the security paying zero in every future state to $\{s_j\}$ and $\mathscr{S}$, then $\mathscr{S}$ satisfies the requirements of a linear space. Proposition 2.1 implies that

$$\beta^i \cdot s_j = \beta^{i'} \cdot s_j \qquad (2.10)$$

for any two individuals i, i' whenever security $s_j \in \mathscr{S}$. Proposition 2.2, where $\mathscr{S} = R^S$, implies that $\beta^i = \beta^{i'} = \beta$ for any two individuals.[6]

The practical significance of Propositions 2.1 and 2.2 is that the structure of security markets, in particular the location and size of the space, matters to the valuation of assets among investors. If $\mathscr{S} = R^S$, a situation we will summarize by saying that markets are "complete," the payment profile of any asset can be valued by reference to a unique set of prices $\beta(\alpha) \alpha = 1, \ldots, S$ which can be inferred from observed prices of traded securities. A security s will have the value $\beta \cdot s$ for any investor. It follows then that a firm contemplating a project with future profile of payments. $s = (\ldots, p_j(\alpha) F_j(K_j, L_j, \alpha), \ldots)$ will want to use the value of the market equivalent $\beta \cdot s$ to measure profitability. This is precisely what has been assumed in Chapter 1.

What happens if $\mathscr{S}$ is not equal to R^S? In this case it may still be the case that the planned project has payoff profile which is in $\mathscr{S}$. If so, Proposition 2.1 says that it can be unanimously valued uniquely among investors. Only when the project is not in $\mathscr{S}$ do we receive no guidance. In that case the firm's project s may be such that $\beta^i \cdot s \neq \beta^{i'} \cdot s$. How the firm resolves the difference of opinion between its shareholders is considered in Chapter 3.

D. Summary

The portfolio decision of the investor was described and its relationship to his consumption choices and utility indicated. The formation of risk prices $\beta^i(\alpha)$ was given, with a description of the relationship between them for different investors. The importance

---

[6] Apply (2.10) for $e_1, \ldots, e_S$.

to investor welfare of the ability to write state dependent contracts was discussed with an example.

E. Bibliographic notes

The basic references on securities and risk sharing are Arrow [1964, 1970]. Pomery [1983] discusses the importance of stock markets to understanding the workings of the general equilibrium trade model under uncertainty. Additional references will be provided after the production side of the model is given in Chapter 3.

3. UNCERTAINTY AND PRODUCTION: SUPPLY

The presence of randomness in firms' output leads to two issues. The first is how to specify the firm's choice between different production plans. The second is to determine what optimality properties the firms' choice rule may have and compare it to other rules. For now we look at the first issue, the production choices of firms.

To see that there is a problem which needs to be resolved, in this chapter we will break the discussion down into four parts depending on alternative assumptions made about the firm in different kinds of risk markets. The classification will coincide with progressively fewer opportunities for investors in the model to share risk. The biographical notes at the end of the chapter will point out which papers have used the alternative approaches.

A. Complete markets and stockholder agreement

If there are S states of nature, the pricing relation (2.5) implies n equations in $\beta^i(1), \ldots, \beta^i(S)$ where n is the number of linearly independent payoff vectors in R^S. If markets are complete ($n = S$) this implies the existence of unique prices for risk $\beta(\alpha)$. That is, $\beta^i(\alpha) = \beta(\alpha)$ for all investors i. When a traded security is an elementary security e_α, then $\beta(\alpha)$ is its market price.

With available spot prices $p_1(\alpha)$, $p_2(\alpha)$ and prices for risk $\beta(\alpha)$, the market value of the firm for any production plan is simply the present value of its future output,

$$\sum_{\alpha} \beta(\alpha)[p_j(\alpha)F_j(K_j, L_j, \alpha)] \qquad (3.1)$$

Maximizing market value less the cost of inputs implies the rule

$$\underset{\{K_j, L_j\}}{\text{Max}} \sum_{\alpha} \beta(\alpha)[p_j(\alpha)F_j(K_j, L_j, \alpha)] - wL_j - rK_j \qquad (3.2)$$

which agrees with profit maximization in a Debreu model (the output vector is $y_j = (F_j(K_j, L_j, 1), \ldots, F_j(K_j, L_j, S), -L_j, -K_j)$ with associated prices $p = (\beta(1)p_j(1), \ldots, \beta(S)p_j(S), w, r))$.

But is the market value maximization rule (3.2) what stockholders want the firm to do and is it in their best interests? The answer to both questions is yes in the same sense that competitive pricetaking behavior is in the interest of owners of firms in a deterministic competitive model. This follows from the fact that a model of uncertainty with complete markets, by re-interpretation, is identical to an appropriate deterministic competitive model. The optimality properties are therefore identical for both. (We will take this up again in Chapter 6.) But what the consumer wants the firm to do depends on his *perceptions* of the market structure. When the market structure is incomplete, these perceptions become crucial to understanding the responses of firms to risk. The following exercise relates the market value maximization rule (3.2) to stockholder welfare.

Writing the Lagrangian for the consumer's portfolio problem,

$$\mathcal{L} = U^i(I^i(1), \ldots, I^i(S); p)$$

$$+ \lambda^i \left[\sum_{j=1}^{2} (\bar{\theta}_j^i - \theta_j^i)P_j - \sum_{j=1}^{2} \bar{\theta}_j^i(rK_j + wL_j) - b^i \right] \qquad (3.3)$$

and totally differentiating with respect to K_1 gives,

$$\frac{1}{\lambda^i} \frac{\partial L}{\partial K_1} = \sum_{\alpha} \beta^i(\alpha) \left[\theta_1^i p_1(\alpha) \frac{\partial F_1}{\partial K_1} + \frac{\partial \theta_1^i}{\partial K_1} p_1(\alpha) F_1 \right.$$

$$\left. + \theta_1^i \frac{\partial p_1(\alpha)}{\partial K_1} F_1 + \omega_1^i(\alpha) \frac{\partial p_1(\alpha)}{\partial K_1} \right]$$

$$+ \sum_{\alpha} \beta^i(\alpha) \left[\theta_2^i p_2(\alpha) \left[\frac{\partial F_2}{\partial K_2} \frac{\partial K_2}{\partial K_1} + \frac{\partial F_2}{\partial L_2} \frac{\partial L_2}{\partial K_1} \right] \right]$$

$$
\begin{aligned}
&+ \frac{\partial \theta_2^i}{\partial K_1} p_2(\alpha) F_2 + \theta_2^i \frac{\partial p_2(\alpha)}{\partial K_1} F_2 + \omega_2^i(\alpha) \frac{\partial p_2(\alpha)}{\partial K_1} \Bigg] \\
&+ \sum_\alpha \beta^i(\alpha) \left[\rho \frac{\partial b^i}{\partial K_1} + b^i \frac{\partial \rho}{\partial K_1} + \rho \frac{\partial b^i}{\partial K_1} + L^i \frac{\partial w}{\partial K_1} \right. \\
&\left. + w \frac{\partial L^i}{\partial K_1} + K^i \frac{\partial r}{\partial K_1} + r \frac{\partial K^i}{\partial K_1} \right] \\
&+ \sum_j \sum_\alpha \frac{\partial U^i / \partial p_j(\alpha)}{\lambda^i} \frac{\partial p_j(\alpha)}{\partial K_1} \\
&+ \sum_j \left((\bar{\theta}_j^i - \theta_j^i) \frac{\partial P_j}{\partial K_1} - \frac{\partial \theta_j^i}{\partial K_1} P_j \right) \\
&- \bar{\theta}_1^i \left(r - \frac{dw}{\partial K_1} L_1 \right) - \bar{\theta}_2^i \left(K_2 \frac{\partial r}{\partial K_1} + r \frac{\partial K_2}{\partial K_1} \right. \\
&\left. + L_2 \frac{\partial w}{\partial K_1} + w \frac{\partial L_2}{\partial K_1} \right) - \frac{\partial b^i}{\partial K_1} \tag{3.4}
\end{aligned}
$$

Equation (3.4) embodies all of the channels by which the welfare of investor i is influenced when firm 1 changes its choice of capital input. By Roy's identity, for example, $\partial U^i / \partial p_j(\alpha) = -x_j^i(\alpha) \partial U^i / \partial I^i(\alpha)$ where $x_j^i(\alpha)$ is i's consumption of good j in state α. The term

$$\sum_\alpha \frac{\partial U^i / \partial p_j(\alpha)}{\lambda^i} \frac{\partial p_j(\alpha)}{\partial K_1}$$

becomes $-\sum \beta^i(\alpha) x_j^i(\alpha) \frac{\partial p_j(\alpha)}{\partial K_1}$ which represents the terms of trade improvement for individual i due to changes in prices induced by ∂K_1. Welfare improves in present value terms, for example, if the price drops $(\partial p_j(\alpha)/\partial K_1 < 0)$ for a commodity which i purchases in state $\alpha (x_j^i(\alpha) > 0)$ since $\beta^i(\alpha) x_j^i(\alpha) \frac{\partial p_j(\alpha)}{\partial K_1} > 0$.

The same kind of price effects are present in the deterministic model since ability to influence prices to the advantage of the owners of a firm represent a form of monopoly power. These effects are ruled out in a competitive model by the assumption of price-taking behavior. Individual agents are too small to have noticeable price influence.

Assuming competitive-like behavior (e.g., agents perceive their influence on prices to be negligible) implies that (3.4) can be simplified by eliminating those terms depending on changes in market prices and the effect that ∂K_1 has on the choices of other firms. From the first order conditions to the consumer's problem (2.5), terms depending on variation in θ_1^i, θ_2^i, and b^i cancel. (3.4) reduces to,

$$\frac{1}{\lambda^i}\frac{\partial U^i}{\partial K_1} = \theta_1^i \left(\sum_\alpha \beta^i(\alpha) p_1(\alpha) \frac{\partial F_1}{\partial K_1} - r \right) + (\bar{\theta}^i - \theta^i)\left[\frac{\partial P_1}{\partial K_1} - r\right]. \quad (3.5)$$

It should be emphasized that (3.5) is not the actual change in welfare for i given a change in K_1 (that is given in (3.4)), but rather the change as it is perceived by i given our assumptions. $(\bar{\theta}_j^i - \theta_j^i)\left(\frac{\partial P_1}{\partial K_1} - r\right)$ is a pure wealth re-distribution term. Insofar as $\bar{\theta}_j^i - \theta_j^i > 0$ it indicates that i is a net seller of claims to firm 1. If the change in K_1 induces a greater increase in market value than the rental cost of the capital to generate it, then i has gained by the ability to sell his asset at a greater net price. If different investors have different perceptions of the change in P_1 then the wealth redistribution terms need not sum to zero. Assuming investors see the same $\partial P_1/\partial K_1$, however, summing (3.5) over all investors implies,

$$\sum_i \frac{1}{\lambda^i}\frac{\partial U^i}{\partial K_1} = \sum_i \theta_j^i \sum_\alpha \beta^i(\alpha) p_1(\alpha) \frac{\partial F_1}{\partial K_1} - r$$

$$= \sum_\alpha \beta(\alpha) p_1(\alpha) \frac{\partial F_1}{\partial K_1} - r \quad (3.6)$$

where the substitution of $\beta(\alpha)$ for $\beta^i(\alpha)$ in (3.6) follows from the existence of complete markets. The same procedure applied to the firm's use of labor implies that,

$$\sum_i 1/\lambda^i \frac{\partial U^i}{\partial L_1} = \sum_\alpha \beta(\alpha) p_1(\alpha) \frac{\partial F_1}{\partial L_1} - w.$$

Comparison of (3.6) with (1.6) and (1.7) shows that they imply maximization of stockholder utility where the change in utility of the investors (in present value currency terms) are summed by the firm.

But we are now in position to answer the first question posed at the start of the section in the affirmative. In the complete markets model $P_j = \sum_\alpha \beta(\alpha) p_j(\alpha) F_j$. Given fixed prices $dP_j = \sum_\alpha \beta(\alpha) p_j(\alpha) dF_j$. Substituting this into (3.5) shows that all *ex ante* stockholders in the firm ($\bar{\theta}_j^i > 0$) are unanimous in wanting the firm to maximize net stock market value. A similar argument for *ex post* stockholders, by considering the change in $U^i(I^i(1), \ldots, I^i(S); p)$, shows that they are in unanimous agreement that the firm should maximize its stock market value P_j. Thus the two groups differ from each other only with respect to the first period inputs which must be paid for by *ex ante* shareholders. It can be shown that stock market value maximization also leads to a Pareto Optimum for the economy as a whole. Thus when markets are complete stock market value maximization is both desired by consumers and optimal in the large.

B. Incomplete markets and stockholder disagreement

In the complete markets model there is no room for disagreement between shareholders because both risk and spot prices $\beta^i(\alpha)$, $p_j(\alpha)$ are identical for all individuals. When markets are incomplete, equality of $\beta^i(\alpha)$ across individuals is no longer guaranteed. As a result, market value maximization is not feasible as a firm rule in general. The fundamental problem is that prices $\beta(\alpha)$ do not exist for calculating a unique market value for all feasible projects. Equation (3.5) continues to show the stockholder's change in welfare for a given change in inputs but it will generally differ from investor to investor.

Assuming that the firm seeks the highest value for the project chosen, regardless of distribution of the value among shareholders, implies that the firm solves the problem,

$$\underset{(K_j, L_j)}{\text{Max}} \sum_i \theta_j^i \left(\sum_\alpha \beta^i(\alpha) p_j(\alpha) F_j \right) - w L_j - r K_j \qquad (3.7)$$

with first order conditions,

$$\sum_i \frac{1}{\lambda^i} \frac{\partial U^i}{\partial K_j} = \sum_i \theta_j^i \left(\sum_\alpha \beta^i(\alpha) p_j(\alpha) \frac{\partial F_j}{\partial K_j} \right) - r \leq 0$$

$$\sum_i \frac{1}{\lambda^i} \frac{\partial U^i}{\partial L_j} = \sum_i \theta_j^i \left(\sum_\alpha \beta^i(\alpha) p_j(\alpha) \frac{\partial F_j}{\partial L_j} \right) - w \leq 0 \qquad (3.8)$$

which reduce to (1.6), (1.7) if $\beta^i(\alpha) = \beta(\alpha)$ for all i. On the other hand, if investors perceive different changes in P_j according to their own risk prices, $dP^i = \sum \beta^i_j(\alpha) p_j(\alpha) \, dF_j$, then the firm rule reduces to,

$$\underset{(k_j, l_j)}{\text{Max}} \sum_i \bar{\theta}^i_j (\sum_\alpha \beta^i(\alpha) p_j(\alpha) F_j) - wL_j - rK_j \qquad (3.7')$$

where *ex post* shareholdings replace the *ex ante* shareholdings in (3.7). First order conditions for (3.7') also reduce to (1.6), (1.7) if $\beta^i(\alpha) = \beta(\alpha)$ for all i. In the absence of complete markets, however, one rule favors *ex ante* investors and the other *ex post*. The equilibria and optimality properties of the model will be different depending on whether firms use (3.7) or (3.7'). The analysis of international trade propositions, however, will be little affected by whichever alternative is used. For purposes of our discussion, we will assume rational expectations by consumers about the effect of input changes on firm prices. Thus all investors use the actual $\partial P_j / \partial K_j$; $\partial P_j / \partial L_j$ generated by the model. Indifference about the distribution of gains among shareholders by the firm then implies rule (3.7). A further discussion of the distinction between rule (3.7) and (3.7') can be found in the references discussed in the bibliographic notes.

C. The special case of spanning

The properties of (3.7) discussed so far are that it is derived from maximization of investor welfare, it applies to choices among any list of potential projects, and if markets are complete, it reduces to profit maximization (and market value maximization) as in the deterministic Debreu-type model. We now discuss one additional feature which relates to the span of the set of traded securities $\mathcal{S}$.

If the vector $p_j \, dF_j$ is a member of $\mathcal{S}$ it implies that the inner product $\beta^i \cdot p_j \, dF_j$ is identical across investors i, even though $\beta^i(\alpha)$ varies with i. The implication is that investors will be unanimous in their preference that the firm maximize its market value, now well-defined, just as in the complete markets case. In fact, there is a similarity in structure between models where spanning applies and complete market models. (See the bibliographic notes.) For now, we will confine ourselves to showing how the equivalence between the inner products $\beta^i \cdot p_j \, dF_j$ leads to market value maximization and discussing one case where it arises.

If $p_j \, dF_j \in \mathcal{S}$ then by definition there are scalars a_{jk} $k = 1, \ldots, n$ such that

$$p_j(\alpha) \frac{\partial F_j(K_j, L_j, \alpha)}{\partial K_j} = \sum_k a_{jk} p_k(\alpha) F_k(K_k, L_k, \alpha), \qquad (3.9)$$

and similarly for $\partial F_j / \partial L_j$. The inner product $\beta^i \cdot p_j \, dF_j$ is then equal to

$$\beta^i \cdot p_j \frac{\partial F_j}{\partial K_j} = \sum_{\alpha=1}^{S} \sum_{k=1}^{n} a_{jk} \beta^i(\alpha) p_k(\alpha) F_k(K_k, L_k, \alpha)$$

$$= \sum_{k=1}^{n} a_{jk} \sum_{\alpha=1}^{S} \beta^i(\alpha) p_k(\alpha) F_k(K_k, L_k, \alpha)$$

$$= \sum_{k=1}^{n} a_{jk} P_k \qquad (3.10)$$

where the second equality follows from re-arrangement of terms and the last from the consumer's first order conditions (2.5). Since $\sum_{k=1}^{n} a_k P_k$ is independent of i, $\beta^i \cdot p_j \, dF_j$ the same for all investors given by the weighted average of market prices P_k.

$p_j \, dF_j$ spanned by traded securities indicates that it is made up of components which are equivalent to traded assets. These have unique market prices which are equal by trade for all consumers. (3.5) and (3.9) then indicate that investors are unanimous in wanting the firm to maximize its market value assuming $\partial P_j / \partial K_j = \sum_\alpha \beta^i(\alpha) p_j(\alpha) \, \partial F_j / \partial K_j$. This is the natural assumption to make as the following special case shows.

Assume that $F_j(K_j, L_j, \alpha) = \phi_j(\alpha) h_j(K_j, L_j)$, i.e., that uncertainty enters as a multiplicative factor. This is a very special assumption because it places exogenous technological restrictions on the firm's production function, but it leads to particularly simple conclusions, as we shall see. The vector of firm output can now be written as $h_j(K_j, L_j)(\phi_j(1), \ldots, \phi_j(S))$ where $h_j(K_j, L_j)$ changes the scale of the output vector, but not its stochastic profile. It is natural to suggest that for two otherwise identical firms the one with the larger size will have larger market value in proportion to its relative scale. Since the firm's output is always a linear combination of itself, (3.9) implies that,

$$\beta^i \cdot p_j \frac{\partial F_j}{\partial K_j} = \frac{\partial h_j / \partial K_j}{h_j} \beta^i \cdot p_j F_j$$

$$= \frac{\partial h_j / \partial K_j}{h_j} p_j \tag{3.10'}$$

showing that the value of output changes in proportion to the scale of operation h_j. The assumption that

$$\frac{\partial P_j / \partial K_j}{p_j} = \frac{\partial h_j / \partial K_j}{h_j} \tag{3.11}$$

is natural given (3.10'). The generalization of (3.10) is

$$\partial P_j / \partial K_j = \sum_{k=1}^{n} a_{jk} P_j. \tag{3.12}$$

In the special case where $a_{jk} = 0$, $j \neq k$, $a_{jk} = \frac{\partial h_j / \partial K_j}{h_j}$ reducing (3.11) to (3.10).

Applying (3.11) to (3.5), spanning implies that investor welfare unanimously rises with net market value $(P_j - wL_j - rK_j)$. If uncertainty is multiplicative, this can be written as

$$(\pi_j h_j(K_j, L_j) - wL_j - rK_j) \tag{3.13}$$

where $\pi_j \equiv \Sigma_\alpha \beta^i(\alpha) p_j(\alpha) \phi_j(\alpha)$. Maximization of (3.13) is then formally identical to profit maximization in the neoclassical 2-good, 2-sector Heckscher–Ohlin model. π_j can be thought of as the price for the composite good or "real security" whose payoffs are $(\phi_j(1) \ldots, \phi_j(S))$.

D. The absence of spanning, the absence of risk sharing

The fact that $p_j \, dF_j \in S$ implies investor unanimity and a well-defined market value maximization rule for firms assuming (3.10), would remain a curiosity except that it plays an important role in understanding the workings of the risk market. Figure 1 represents three cases classified by the degree of risk sharing determined by $\mathscr{S}$.

In each case, the issues raised in this chapter can be discussed

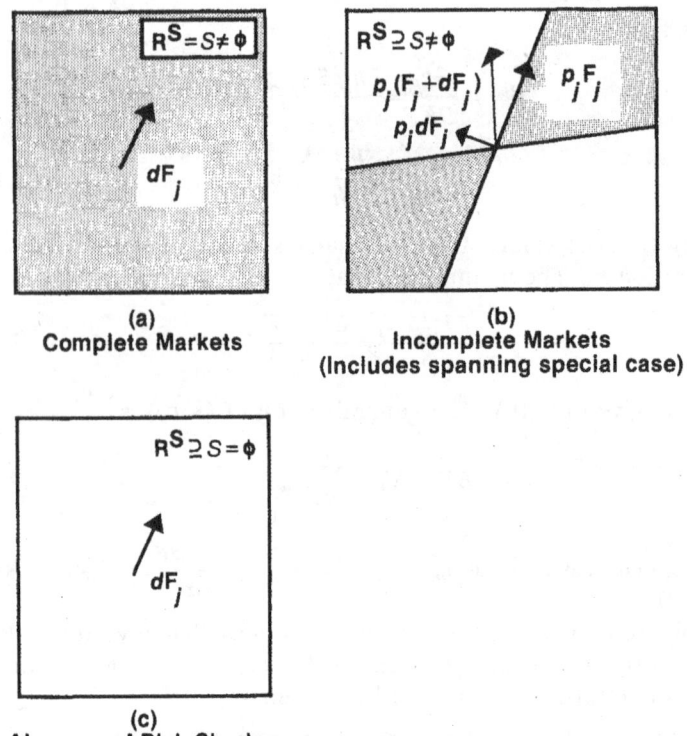

FIGURE 3.1 Representation of alternative assumptions about markets for risk.

with respect to the corresponding diagram. In Section A we discussed production with perfect risk sharing in complete markets. We now introduce the opposite extreme of no markets for sharing risk and relate it to the other cases. We do so by the classification given by $\mathscr{S}$, the span of traded securities.

In Figure 1(a) $\mathscr{S} = R^S$; there are complete markets for sharing risk. The implication is that $\beta^i(\alpha) = \beta(\alpha)$ for all i (marginal rates of transformation for income across states are equalized across consumers). As a result, any change in production dF_j can be uniquely valued and investors are unanimous in wanting the firm to maximize its market value. The model achieves a Pareto Optimum.

By contrast, in Figure 1(b), $\mathscr{S}$ is a proper subset of R^S (the linear subset $\mathscr{S}$ is represented by the shaded area). $p_j F_j$, the production vector of firm j, is drawn, as well as the feasible direction of change $p_j\,dF_j$. Since markets are incomplete $\{\beta^i(\alpha)\}$ vary from investor to investor, but the inner product of β^i with an element of $\mathscr{S}$ is the same for all i. Investors are no longer unanimous in their preferences among alternative projects of the firm, except in the event that $p_j\,dF_j$ is contained in $\mathscr{S}$. Profit maximization and market value maximization is also no longer defined except for $p_j\,dFj$ in $\mathscr{S}$. If $p_j\,dF_j$ is not in $\mathscr{S}$, (3.5) indicates that pure wealth effects (the second term on the right hand side) as well as differences of opinion about the value of the project at given prices, cause different opinions about the desirability of projects. The market equilibrium no longer achieves a Pareto Optimum (we will discuss weaker forms of optimality which it does achieve in Chapter 5). In fact, through its decision the firm partially determines the size and location of $\mathscr{S}$ as a subset of R^S. This is because investors trade shares of firms and a change in the asset traded changes the set of contracts available for spreading risk. Chapter 2 showed that the ability to write various contracts affected the market's ability to spread risk. We would expect, therefore, that part of the disagreement between investors in general relates to differing perceptions about what set of contracts would best suit their risk-spreading needs. This notion will be made precise in Chapter 7.

Last, turning to Figure 1(c) consider the opposite polar case to complete markets. Here the space spanned by the returns of traded securities is the null set. In other words, there is no trading of assets. In this case the entrepreneur operating each firm must decide how to choose among alternative investments in the absence of any information about the risk prices of the other individuals. The only reasonable assumption is that the owner of firm j solves the problem,

$$\underset{\{K_j,\,L_j\}}{\text{Max}}\ U^i(I^i(1),\ldots,I^i(S);p)$$

$$\text{s.t.}\ I^i(\alpha) = p_j(\alpha)F_j(K_j, L_j, \alpha) - \rho r K_j - \rho w L_j + \rho r K^i + \rho w L^i$$

$$+ \sum_j p_j(\alpha)\omega_j^i(\alpha). \tag{3.14}$$

(3.14) is related to the earlier objective functions by setting $\bar{\theta}_j^i$, θ_j^i and b^i identically equal to zero in (3.3) and replacing the formula for $I^i(\alpha)$ by the constraint in (3.14). Assuming competitive-like behavior and price-taking with respect to spot prices as before,

$$\frac{1}{\lambda^i} dU^i = \sum_\alpha \beta^i(\alpha) p_j(\alpha) \, dF_j - r \, dK_j - w \, dL_j \qquad (3.15)$$

where λ^i is the marginal utility of initial wealth.[7] Solution of (3.14) therefore implies the first order conditions,

$$\sum_\alpha \beta^i(\alpha) p_j(\alpha) \frac{\partial F_j}{\partial K_j} - r \leq 0$$

$$\sum_\alpha \beta^i(\alpha) p_j(\alpha) \frac{\partial F_j}{\partial K_j} - w \leq 0 \qquad (3.16)$$

which can be compared to (3.8). In the special case where the enterpreneur is risk neutral, $\beta^i(\alpha)$ is simply the subjective probability of state α and (3.14) reduces to maximization of expected profits. The intermediate case between no markets for risk where (3.16) applies and complete markets for risk where (3.2) applies, is the case where $\mathcal{S}$ is neither R^S nor ϕ and (3.7) applies.

The importance of $\mathcal{S}$ follows from the constraints that it imposes on the relationship between $\beta^i(\alpha)$ across investors. The validity of the traditional theorems of international trade theory are sensitive to the maturity and extent of the markets for risk. The continuum suggested by Figure 1 will be useful in discussing the validity or falsity of the traditional trade propositions as a function of the degree of risk-spreading opportunities in the risk markets. This is taken up in Chapter 4.

D. Summary

With production uncertainty and incomplete markets it is not clear what objective the firm should pursue in choosing its production plan. Investor unanimity is no longer guaranteed, but depends heavily on the assumptions made about competition and the investors' perception of the effect of the firm's action on its market value. Two natural alternatives were described which imply two related choice rules for the firm. The importance of the span of traded securities for firm decision making was enunciated.

---

[7] The assets of the investor are $wL^i + rK^i = a^i$. $\partial U^i / \partial a^i \equiv \lambda^i$.

E. Bibliographic notes

The sociology of investor unanimity and the firm's decision making under uncertainty has been considered in a number of papers in both the finance, pure theory, and trade literature. Papers dealing with the unanimity question include Diamond [1967], Ekern and Wilson [1974], Radner [1974], Leland [1974], Nielsen [1976], Grossman and Stiglitz [1980], DeAngelo [1981] and Grinols [1984a] among others. Drèze [1974] and Grossman and Hart [1979] have considered the optimality properties of the alternative rules (3.7) and (3.7') for the firm. The model of Section B has been described in the trade context by Grinols [1985a]. The model of Section C with multiplicative production uncertainty has been described by Batra [1974], Helpman and Razin [1978], Baron and Forsythe [1979], Pomery [1979] and Young [1984]. Batra and Young deal with the model in the case where firms are wholly owned by entrepreneurs with no stock markets for trading risk. Helpman and Razin, Baron and Forsythe, and Pomery describe the model with markets for equity shares available. Comparative statics properties of production under uncertainty are considered by Batra [1974], Kemp and Liviatan [1973], Kemp [1976], and Kemp and Ohta [1979].

4. THE THEOREMS OF INTERNATIONAL TRADE THEORY

Among its most basic interests, international trade theory is concerned with the relationships between commodity prices and factor rewards, factor endowments and production, the pattern of trade, and the effect of trade on prices, factor rewards and welfare. Chapter 3 considered the general equilibrium relationship between spot prices, risk prices and the production decisions of firms. In this chapter we take up the effect of uncertainty on the four major theorems of international trade, the Stolper–Samuelson Theorem, the Rybczynski Theorem, the Factor Price Equilization Theorem, and the Heckscher–Ohlin Theorem. The first two of these are "one-sided" results in that they deal with mechanisms operating in one country of the model at a time; whereas the Factor Price Equalization Theorem and the Heckscher–Ohlin Theorem deal simultaneously with conditions in both countries in world trade. We will also discuss the effect of price changes on output. The gains from trade will be considered in Chapter 5.

The theme which emerges from the analysis of the four theorems of trade is their sensitivity to the nature and extent of risk-sharing opportunities available in the market. On the least developed side of the scale is an economy which has no organized exchanges for risky assets. In such an economy, none of the traditional theorems need apply in any useful way, while in an economy with complete markets all four theorems are valid for appropriate generalizations. Intermediate to these extremes are situations where national risk markets exist, but are incomplete, and cases where international risk markets exist linking national stock exchanges, but are incomplete. In general, international trade in securities is a necessary, but not sufficient, condition for generalizations of the relevant theorems to apply. The most important feature is the nature of the risk market itself.

A. The Stolper–Samuelson Theorem

In the deterministic model, the Stolper–Samuelson Theorem states that a change in relative (spot) prices p_1/p_2 will raise the real reward of the factor used intensively in industry 1 and lower the real reward of the other factor. Consider the case where labor is used intensively by industry 1 (that is, $k_1 < k_2$ where $k_j = K_j/L_j$). Following Jones, the Stolper–Samuelson Theorem says

$$\hat{r} < \hat{p}_2 < \hat{p}_1 < \hat{w} \\ \hat{r} > \hat{p}_2 > \hat{p}_1 > \hat{w} \tag{4.1}$$

where $\hat{}$ denotes percentage change in a variable. Since the percentage change in the wage rate is higher than the percentage increase in the price of either good, the real wage rises in terms of either price. In considering this theorem under uncertainty two issues arise. First, what is the appropriate generalization when risk *and* spot prices $\beta(\alpha)$, $p_j(\alpha)$ are present and typically vary with the state of nature. And second, will the generalization be valid for a given market structure (complete markets, incomplete markets, absence of risk spreading).[8] In the case of the Stolper–Samuelson Theorem we will consider two possible generalizations, one where risk prices play a role in the statement of the theorem and one where they do not. For both versions write the first order conditions for factor demand,

$$r = \sum_i \theta_j^i \sum_\alpha \beta^i(\alpha) p_j(\alpha) \frac{\partial F_j}{\partial K_j} \qquad j = 1, 2$$
$$w = \sum_i \theta_j^i \sum_\alpha \beta^i(\alpha) p_j(\alpha) \frac{\partial F_j}{\partial L_j} \qquad j = 1, 2. \qquad (4.2)$$

As discussed in Chapter 3, if $\beta^i(\alpha) = \beta(\alpha)$ (4.2) becomes the first order condition for factor allocation if markets are perfect. If $\theta_j^i = 0$ for all i but one, (3.2) becomes the relevant expression for the model with no risk markets. In between, (3.2) applies for the case of incomplete markets. A standard assumption in the deterministic model is that production functions are homogeneous of degree one in K_j and L_j. Assuming homogeneity of degree one in inputs for F_j for given α, (4.2) implies

$$dP_1' = \sum_\alpha d(\beta_1(\alpha) p_1(\alpha)) F_1(K_1, L_1, \alpha) = K_1 \, dr + L_1 \, dw$$
$$dP_2' = \sum_\alpha d(\beta_2(\alpha) p_2(\alpha)) F_2(K_2, L_2, \alpha) = K_2 \, dr + L_2 \, dw \qquad (4.4)$$

where $\beta_j(\alpha) \equiv \sum_i \theta_j^i \beta^i(\alpha)$ and dP_1', dP_2' are used to denote changes in P_1, P_2 for fixed levels of output F_j.[9]

Direct inspection of (4.4) shows that changes in both $p_j(\alpha)$ and $\beta_j(\alpha)$ determine changes in r and w. Moreover, real rewards are no longer uniquely defined since with uncertainty present there are more commodities and hence more real wages to consider. Several obvious possibilities for real wages are $w/\beta_j(\alpha)p_j(\alpha)$, $w/p_j(\alpha)$, w/r, and w relative to an index of commodity prices over states of

---

[8] We will also sometimes consider the case where production decisions are spanned by the traded securities, even though this places exogenous restrictions on production technology.

[9] Homogeneity of degree one implies $F_j = \frac{\partial F_j}{\partial L_j} L_j + \frac{\partial F_j}{\partial K_j} K_j$. From (4.2) $\sum_\alpha \beta_j(\alpha) p_j(\alpha) F_j = rK_j + wL_j$, differentiating this, using $\sum_\alpha \beta_j(\alpha) p_j(\alpha) \, dF_j - r \, dK_j - w \, dL_j = 0$ gives (4.4).

nature. In the latter case, if the prices of, say, automobiles are random over states of nature and General Motors produces 10 million cars on average one might want to know how one's wage rate has changed with respect to the cost of purchasing one ten-millionth of General Motors current output. If $F_1(K_1, L_1, \alpha)$ is automobile output this is equivalent to asking how w compares to the cost of purchasing $10^{-7} \cdot (F_1(K_1, L_1, 1), \ldots, F_1(K_1, L_1, S))$. From (2.5) we know this quantity of output has current market price of $10^{-7} \sum_\alpha \beta_1(\alpha) p_1(\alpha) F_1(K_1, L_1, \alpha) = 10^{-7} P_1$. Hence the natural comparison is between $\hat{w}$ and $\hat{P}_1'$ where $\hat{P}_1'$ denotes the percentage change dP_1'/P_1.

Having identified four alternative measures of the real wage (the real return to capital is treated analogously) we need to consider the statement of the theorem. In the deterministic model commodity prices were changed to see what the effect would be on real factor rewards. Commodities in this model, however, are state dependent. Choosing a numeraire only fixes one price. We could therefore consider changing future spot prices $p_1(\alpha)$ (resp. $\beta^i(\alpha)p_1(\alpha)$) relative to $p_2(\alpha)$ ($\beta^i(\alpha)p_2(\alpha)$) say, for each state of nature or consider changing the relative indexes $\sum_\alpha \beta_j(\alpha) p_j(\alpha) F_j$. The latter considers the change in price of the market's average output.

The following argument shows that the Stolper–Samuelson Theorem stated in terms of future spot prices fails but that a version written in terms of the current price of output is valid. To construct the simplest possible case let there be a single consumer (or equivalently multiple identical consumer) with indirect von Neumann–Morgenstern utility functions

$$V(I, p) = \sum_\alpha \pi_\alpha U(I^i(\alpha); p) \qquad (4.5)$$

where π_α is the probability of state α. Production satisfies

$$F_1(K_1, L_1, \alpha) = \alpha h_1(K_1, L_1)$$
$$F_2(K_2, L_2, \alpha) = h_2(K_2, L_2) \qquad (4.6)$$

so that production of good 2 is deterministic. h_1 and h_2 are homogeneous of degree 1 in K and L. Industry 1 is capital intensive. Output of firm 1 given K_1, L_1 is random, but because α enters multiplicatively the risk characteristics of the output stream

UNCERTAINTY AND THEORY OF INTERNATIONAL TRADE 31

are fixed by the values taken by α, and h_1 only determines scale of operation. Initially relative spot prices are fixed and given by $p_1 = p_2 = 1$. Assume now that p_1 rises with p_2 fixed. For fixed prices $\beta_j(\alpha) \equiv \beta^i(\alpha)$ for all i, h_1 will rise and h_2 will fall. For the economy as a whole this means that the quantity of the risky asset has risen and the quantity of the riskless asset has fallen. With higher prices investor portfolios have increased in value. If the increased wealth leads investors to demand more of the risky asset and less of the safe asset in precisely the amounts supplied by the market, asset equilibrium prevails. Totally differentiate (4.2) to get,

$$
\begin{aligned}
dr &= \sum_\alpha \beta_1(\alpha)p_1(\alpha)f_1'' \, dk_1 + \sum_\alpha d[\beta_1(\alpha)p_1(\alpha)]f_1' \\
dr &= \sum_\alpha \beta_2(\alpha)p_2(\alpha)f_2'' \, dk_2 + \sum_\alpha d[\beta_2(\alpha)p_2(\alpha)]f_2' \\
dw &= -k_1 \sum_\alpha \beta_1(\alpha)p_1(\alpha)f_1'' \, dk_1 + \sum_\alpha d[\beta_1(\alpha)p_1(\alpha)][f_1 - k_1 f_1'] \\
dw &= -k_2 \sum_\alpha \beta_2(\alpha)p_2(\alpha)f_2'' \, dk_2 + \sum_\alpha d[\beta_2(\alpha)p_2(\alpha)][f_2 - k_2 f_2']
\end{aligned}
\tag{4.7}
$$

where $k_j = K_j/L_j$, $f_j = F_j(k_j, 1, \alpha)$ and superscript $'$ denotes differentiation with respect to k_j. Writing (4.4) in the example at hand,

$$\sum_\alpha \beta_1(\alpha)\alpha \, dp_1 h_1(K_1, L_1) = K_1 \, dr + L_1 \, dw$$

$$0 = K_2 \, dr + L_2 \, dw \tag{4.8}$$

implies that

$$\binom{dr}{dw} = \frac{(P_1/L_1)dp_1}{(k_1 - k_2)} \binom{1}{-k_2}. \tag{4.9}$$

(4.7) and (4.9) together imply that $dk_1 < 0$, and $dk_2 < 0$. Thus $\hat{r} > \hat{p}_1 > \hat{p}_2 > \hat{w}$ because falling k_1, k_2 lowers the marginal product of labor and raises the marginal product of capital.[10] It follows in the

---

[10] $(k_1 - k_2) > 0$ by assumption that industry 1 is the capital intensive industry. Thus $dr > 0$, $dw < 0$. Since $\beta_j(\alpha) > 0$, $dp_1 > 0$, $dp_2 = 0$, $f_j'' < 0$ (4.7) implies dk_1, $dk_2 < 0$. w/p_2 equals the marginal product of labor in industry 2, and r/p_1 equals $(\sum_\alpha \beta_1(\alpha)\alpha)\frac{\partial h_1}{\partial K_1}$ in industry 1, hence an increase in $\partial h_1/\partial K_1$ implies $\hat{r} > \hat{p}_1 > \hat{p}_2 = 0 > \hat{w}$.

simple example that changes in $w/\beta_j(\alpha)p_j$, w/p_j and w/r moves in the same direction.

However, let us drop the assumption that investors are willing to increase their risky holdings as their portfolio wealth grows. Inspection of (4.4) and (4.7) suggests that changes in $\beta_j(\alpha)$ induced by excess supply of the risky asset at original risk prices could lead to an increase in k_1, k_2 and the reverse effect on real factor rewards. In the case at hand this is verified by totally differentiating the first order conditions in the semi-reduced form,

$$P_1(f_1 - k_1 f'_1) \sum_\alpha \pi_\alpha \left(\frac{U'}{\sum_\alpha \pi_\alpha U'}\right) \alpha = p_2(f_2 - k_2 f'_2)$$

$$p_1 f'_1 \sum_\alpha \pi_\alpha \left(\frac{U'}{\sum_\alpha \pi_\alpha U'}\right) = p_2 f'_2 \qquad (4.10)$$

$$l_1(k_1 - k_2) = k - k_2$$

where $l_1 = L_1/L$, using the formula for income,

$$I(\alpha) = p_1 \alpha f_1(k_1) l_1 L + p_2 f_2(k_2)(1 - l_1)L.$$

Solving for $dk_1/d(p_2/p_1)$, $dk_2/d(p_2/p_1)$ shows that both depend on

$$\left(\sum_\alpha \pi_\alpha \frac{U''}{(\sum_\alpha \pi_\alpha U'')} \alpha f'_1 - r\right)$$

which can be positive or negative. A positive value implies $dk_1, dk_2 < 0$ (the Stolper–Samuelson-type response) but a large enough negative number can cause $dk_1, dk_2 > 0$.[11]

Unless changes in risk prices are taken into account there is no hope that changes in factor rewards can be predicted from changes in future spot prices. In fact, however, there is no real reason why we would want to. For consider that the change in relative commodity prices in the deterministic model involves prices which consumers will actually pay for purchases of the commodity as well as the variables which determine the decision to produce. In the model with uncertainty, the price $p_1(\alpha)$ may never be seen by the

---

[11] Batra [1975] derives the formula for dk_1, dk_2 in his book. We will discuss another example of changes in risk prices $\beta_j(\alpha)$ moving to overturn the normal effect of spot prices in Chapter 6 when the effects of a tariff under uncertainty are considered.

consumer. *Ex ante* he faces a menu of potential future spot prices. What we are interested in is the effect on his real earning power of a change which shifts his menu in a particular direction with the greater importance of some potential outcomes over others already taken into account. The logical candidate is the Laspeyres price index $\sum \beta_j(\alpha)p_j(\alpha)F_j$, already introduced, which is effectively the price of the real equity or composite commodity which pays $p_j(\alpha)F_j(K_j, L_j, \alpha)$ in state α. No restriction needs to be made on the movement in individual prices $p_j(\alpha)$ because the weighting $\beta_j(\alpha)F_j$ already weights different prices for their relative importance.

We now state the following proposition, discussing its importance for complete markets, incomplete markets, and the case with no risk spreading afterwards.

PROPOSITION 4.1 (*Stolper–Samuelson–Price Magnification*) *In the Model of Chapters 1 and 2 with firm choices described by (3.7), if both goods are produced using positive capital and labor, and industry 1 is capital intensive relative to industry 2, then $\hat{P}_1' > \hat{P}_2'$ implies,*

$$\hat{r} > \hat{P}_1' > \hat{P}_2' > \hat{w}.$$

Proof Rewriting Eq. (4.4)

$$\begin{pmatrix} \hat{P}_1' \\ \hat{P}_2' \end{pmatrix} = \begin{pmatrix} \dfrac{rk_1}{P_1} & \dfrac{wL_1}{P_1} \\ \dfrac{rk_2}{P_2} & \dfrac{wL_2}{P_2} \end{pmatrix} \begin{pmatrix} \hat{r} \\ \hat{w} \end{pmatrix}$$

Solving,

$$\hat{r} = \frac{(k_1 + w/r)\hat{P}_1' - (k_2 + w/r)\hat{P}_2'}{k_1 - k_2},$$

$$\hat{w} = \frac{w/r(k_1 + w/r)\hat{P}_2' - k_2(k_1 + w/r)\hat{P}_1'}{w/r(k_1 - k_2)}$$

$$\hat{r} - \hat{P}_1' = \frac{(k_2 + w/r)}{k_1 - k_2}(\hat{P}_1' - \hat{P}_2') > 0$$

$$\hat{w} - \hat{P}_2' = -\frac{k_2(k_1 + w/r)}{\dfrac{w}{r}(k_1 - k_2)}(\hat{P}_1' - \hat{P}_2') < 0, \quad \text{since} \quad k_1 - k_2 > 0$$

by the assumption of industry capital intensities. ∎

Proposition 4.1 is general in that it applies regardless of the sophistication of the markets for risk spreading. It is valid if risk markets are complete, incomplete, or non-existent. Existence of complete markets simply assures that individual risk prices are equal across agents $\beta^i(\alpha) = \beta_j(\alpha) = \beta(\alpha)$ for some $\beta(\alpha)$ for all i, j. However, equality is not required for the proposition. When markets do not exist in equity trade (θ_j^i) became either 0 or 1. But, again, specific values of θ_j^i are not required for the proposition.

When markets are imperfect, the above changes in real prices are no longer sufficient to determine welfare changes to the household, even though they are formally similar to price relations which directly determine welfare in the deterministic model. Deviations between $\beta_j(\alpha)$ and $\beta^i(\alpha)$ are the cause of the potential divergence between price movements and welfare.[12] In this sense, one of the reasons for considering real factor rewards in the first place has been lost. Chapter 7 considers in detail the measurement of the welfare consequences of comparative statics changes.

As a final observation, which applies for this section and the rest of the chapter, if markets are complete the model of uncertainty is formally equivalent to a deterministic model where goods have the market prices $\beta(\alpha)p_j(\alpha)$ and production is joint. Firm j jointly produces the set of goods classified by j and state α in the quantities $F_j(K_j, L_j, \alpha)$. Just as slaughtering a sheep produces wool and mutton in given proportion, the choice of (K_j, L_j) produces outputs in given proportions. The Stolper–Samuelson Theorem, Proposition 4.1, therefore also applies to the joint production model as well. This equivalence has been noted by Chang, Ethier and Kemp [1980].

The Rybczynski Theorem

The Rybczynski Theorem in the deterministic model states that an increase in the supply of a factor at fixed output prices will lead to an increase in the equilibrium output of the good which uses that factor intensively and a decrease in the output of the other good. Since resources from the contracting industry go to the expanding

---

[12] When markets are perfect, or when a firm is owned by a single entrepreneur, $\beta^i(\alpha) = \beta_j(\alpha)$ and this difference is removed.

industry, the percentage expansion in output is greater than the percentage growth of the factor, and since the other industry is contracting, its percentage growth is below the growth rate of the second factor. The surprising features are the percentage magnification and that both goods do not expand their output.

With the introduction of uncertainty the question again arises as to how the theorem should be generalized. Should prices $p_j(\alpha)$ or prices $\beta_j(\alpha)p_j(\alpha)$ be held fixed in the statement of the theorem. If prices $p_j(\alpha)$ are held fixed, but $\beta_j(\alpha)$ are free to vary, the same problem with portfolio demand arises to invalidate the generalization to uncertainty as occurred in the Stopler–Samuelson theorem. Suppose in the example of Section A that the risky industry is intensive in the factor which has increased. At fixed risk prices $\beta_j(\alpha)$ increased output leads to increased portfolio wealth. To satisfy the statement of the theorem output in the risky industry should expand. But this requires investors to hold a greater percentage of the risky asset in their portfolio. If they do not wish to do so, this could induce changes in risk prices moving production in the direction demanded by portfolio balance, negating the theorem. Notice that this possibility arises in essentially the same form in the deterministic model. If prices are not fixed, demand for output might not agree with output levels generated by the theorem and the interaction of demand and supply could lead to a movement in output prices inducing production shifts in the opposite direction specified by the theorem. In the example of Section (A) total differentiation of (4.10) with respect to K, L for fixed p shows that the direction of output change can be positive or negative depending on the magnitude of

$$\left(\sum_\alpha \pi_\alpha \frac{U''}{(\sum_\alpha \pi_\alpha U'')} \alpha f_1 - r \right)$$

which is of either sign. Controlling for demand effects, as in the deterministic model, by controlling for risk prices restores the Rybczynski theorem as the following proposition shows.

PROPOSITION 4.2 (*Rybczynski-Quantity Magnification*) *In the model of Proposition 4.1 if both goods are produced using capital and labor, and industry 1 is capital intensive relative to industry 2, then*

$d\beta_j(\alpha)p_j(\alpha) = 0$, and $\hat{K} > \hat{L}$ imply that

$$\hat{P}_1 > \hat{K} > \hat{L} > \hat{P}_2 \quad \text{and}$$
$$\hat{F}_1(K_1, L_1, \alpha) > \hat{K} > \hat{L} > \hat{F}_2(K_2, L_2, \alpha).$$

Proof Form Eq. (4.4) $\hat{r} = \hat{w} = 0$. From (4.7) this implies $dk_1 = dk_2 = 0$. The full employment conditions for capital and labor $L_1 + L_2 = L$, $K_1 + K_2 = K$ then imply

$$\hat{l}_1 = \frac{k}{l_1(k_1 - k_2)}\hat{k}, \quad \hat{l}_2 = \frac{-l_1}{l_2}\hat{l}_1 < 0, \quad \hat{l}_1 - \hat{k} = \frac{k_2}{l_1(k_1 - k_2)}\hat{k} > 0$$

where $k = K/L$. Writing

$$F_1(K_1, L_1, \alpha) = K\left(\frac{l_1}{k}\right)f_1(k_1), \qquad F_2(K_2, L_2, \alpha) = Ll_2 f_2(k_2)$$

implies that

$$\hat{F}_1(K_1, L_1, \alpha) = \hat{K} + (\hat{l}_1 - \hat{k}) > \hat{K}$$
$$\hat{F}_2(K_2, L_2, \alpha) = \hat{L} + \hat{l}_2 < \hat{L}.$$

Since

$$\hat{P}_j = \sum_\alpha \frac{\beta_j(\alpha)p_j(\alpha)F_j(K_j, L_j, \alpha)}{P_j} \hat{F}_j$$
$$= \hat{F}_j \left(\sum_\alpha \frac{\beta_j(\alpha)p_j(\alpha)F_j(K_j, L_j, \alpha)}{P_j}\right)$$
$$= \hat{F}_j \text{ the result follows.} \blacksquare$$

If $\hat{K} > \hat{L} = 0$, the statement of the theorem reduces to the Rybczynski-type case where one output increases and the other declines. Notice that the theorem is true for relative output changes *state by state* as well as for the Laspeyres index of output $\sum_\alpha \beta_j(\alpha)p_j(\alpha)F_j(K_j, L_j, \alpha)$ weighted by initial prices $\beta_j(\alpha)p_j(\alpha)$. This index, of course, is the market value of firm j's traded security. Since no use was made of differences in market structure generating $\beta_j(\alpha)$, Proposition (4.1) is true for the model with complete markets, incomplete markets, or absence of markets for risk spreading.

C. Factor price equalization

In the deterministic model the Stolper–Samuelson theorem asserts that the reward to the factor used intensively by the commodity

UNCERTAINTY AND THEORY OF INTERNATIONAL TRADE   37

whose price is lowered by trade will fall and vice versa for the factor used intensively in the other industry. The movement of commodity prices to a common set of values worldwide then suggests the tendency for factor rewards to move towards a common value as well. The Factor Price Equalization Theorem asserts that this tendency is perfect, leading to 100 percent equalization of factor rewards.

The validity of Propositions 4.1 and 4.2 suggests the possibility for factor price equalization using the following reasoning. Starting from the initial world trade equilibrium, hold prices $\beta_j(\alpha), p_j(\alpha)$ constant while moving the total capital to labor ratio k in each country to the world average level. In the final position both countries have identical prices and capital-labor ratios, hence they must have the same wage rates and rental rates. According to (4.2) $\hat{w} = \hat{r} = 0$ for this move, just as in the Rybczynski Theorem. It follows that factor prices must have been equal initially.

Inspection of this argument reveals the possibility of flaws at two places. First, it is required that prices must be the same in the two locations and second, $\hat{w}$ and $\hat{r}$ must be zero throughout the move. Failure at either point would invalidate the proof. With respect to prices and $\hat{w}$ and $\hat{r}$ it matters what degree of risk-spreading is available in the markets, intra-country and inter-country. We will examine the different possibilities in turn by first considering the requirements for global univalence and then for local univalence.

Global univalence and factor price equalization. From the first order conditions for the firm,

$$\sum_\alpha \beta_1(\alpha) p_1(\alpha) f_1' - \sum_\alpha \beta_2(\alpha) p_2(\alpha) f_2' = 0$$

$$\sum_\alpha \beta_1(\alpha) p_1(\alpha) [f_1 - k_1 f_1'] - \sum_\alpha \beta_2(\alpha) p_2(\alpha) [f_2 - k_2 f_2'] = 0 \quad (4.10)$$

with the associated Jacobean matrix,

$$J(k_1, k_2) = \begin{pmatrix} A(k_1, k_2) & B(k_1, k_2) \\ -k_1 A(k_1, k_2) & -k_2 B(k_1, k_2) \end{pmatrix}$$

where

$$A(k_1, k_2) = \sum_\alpha \beta_1(\alpha) p_1(\alpha) f_1''$$

$$B(k_1, k_2) = \sum_\alpha \beta_2(\alpha) p_2(\alpha) f_2''.$$

If (a) no principal minors of $J(k_1, k_2)$ vanish on R_+^2, or if (b) the determinant of J is not equal to zero and A and B do not change sign on R_+^2, the solution to (4.10) is globally unique. In the deterministic model $A = f_1''(k_1) < 0$, $B = f_2''(k_2) < 0$ so that neither changes sign on R_+^2 and the first principal minor of J is always negative. The requirement that the determinant of J be nonzero then reduces to $k_1 - k_2 \neq 0$. The absence of factor intensity reversals therefore implies a unique set of factor prices for each set of commodity prices because marginal products of factors are equalized across countries with equalization of the capital intensities k_1, k_2. The following lemma in the case of uncertainty is immediate.

LEMMA 4.1 *If the present discounted value of factor marginal products across states of nature,*

$$\sum_\alpha \beta_j(\alpha) p_j(\alpha) f_j', \sum_\alpha \beta_j(\alpha) p_j(\alpha)(f_j - k_j f_j'),$$

respectively, are equal across countries, then factor prices are equal across countries.

PROPOSITION 4.3 (Factor Price Equalization) *In the model of Proposition (4.2) let condition a or b hold. Then factor price equalization occurs for countries A and B if the value of their state dependent marginal products lie in the space spanned by the returns of internationally traded securities.*

Proof Let $s_k = (s_k(1), \ldots, s_k(\alpha), \ldots, s_k(S)) \in R^S$ be the return to a traded security, Then $p_j(\alpha) f_j'' = \sum_k a_{jk} s_k$ and $p_j(\alpha)(f_j - k_j f_j') = \sum_k b_{jk} s_k$, $j = 1$, for some coefficients $a_{jk}(k_1)$, $b_{jk}(k_2)$ by hypothesis of spanning.

If follows that

$$\sum_\alpha \beta_j(\alpha) p_j(\alpha) f_j' = \sum_k \left(\sum_\alpha \beta_j(\alpha) p_j(\alpha) s_k \right) a_{jk}(k_1)$$
$$= \sum_k P_k a_{jk}(k_1) \qquad (4.11)$$
$$\sum_\alpha \beta_j(\alpha) p_j(\alpha)(f_j - k_j f_j') = \sum_k P_k b_{jk}(k_2)$$

and system (4.10) is identical for all trading countries producing goods 1 and 2. Condition (a) or (b) implies the system is globally univalent, hence k_1, k_2 are equal across countries. Since marginal products depend only on k_1, k_2 lemma 4.1 gives the result. ∎

COROLLARY 4.3 (Factor Price Equalization) *Assume international trade in securities and condition (a) or (b) holds for each trading country. If markets are complete or production uncertainty is multiplicative, then factor price equalization occurs.*

Proof Both results follow from Proposition 4.3. In the former case markets are complete so marginal products must lie in the space spanned by traded securities. In the latter case, $f_i(k_j, \alpha) = \phi_j(\alpha)h_j(k_j)$, $h_j' > 0$, $h_j'' < 0$ for some multiplicative factor, $\phi_j(\alpha)$, implies that $f_j' = \phi_j(\alpha)h_j(k_j)(h'/h_j) = (h_j'/h_j)f_j$ is spanned by itself. ∎

Notice that Proposition 4.3 does not assert that factor price equalization will generally occur (in fact it generally will not) but only gives conditions under which it will occur. Helpman and Razin [1978] argue, for example, that international trade in securities is the crucial element needed to cause equalization of the factor prices. Proposition 4.3 suggests instead that the important element is not international trade in securities but rather the size of the span of traded security returns relative to the state-dependent factor marginal products. It is possible to have international trade in securities and not have factor price equalization even when condition (a) or (b) for global univalence holds. The reason is that prices $\beta_j(\alpha)$ may differ from country to country even with international trade in securities. Different prices imply a different system (4.10) for each country and hence different factor prices. Only if marginal products happen to lie in the space spanned by returns of internationally traded securities is system (4.10) guaranteed to be the same across countries. In that case, univalence gives the result. To summarize, under uncertainty there are two conditions which must be met for global factor price equalization instead of one condition under certainty. The system (4.10) must be globally univalent (also required under certainty) and the value of the marginal product must be spanned by the return of traded securities (automatically satisfied under certainty) in order for (4.10) to be the same set of equations across countries. Otherwise, cross-country differences in risk prices $\beta_j(\alpha)$ cause (4.10) to represent different equations across countries. Univalence of different (4.10) systems would then guarantee factor price *non*-equalization except by chance.

Factor price equalization in general. The previous arguments for factor price equalization dealt with sufficient but not necessary conditions for factor price equalization. It is possible to have factor price equalization without condition (a) or (b). In this section we drop the requirement for global univalence.

If the determinant of J is non-zero, the solution to (4.10) is locally unique but not necessarily globally unique. Let (k_1, k_2) and (k'_1, k'_2) be solutions for (4.10) satisfying the full employment conditions (1.10) and (1.11) for two nonspecialized countries engaged in international trade. Define a cone of diversification to be the span of a set of vectors of the type $\binom{1}{k_1}, \binom{1}{k_2}$ for weights $l_1, 1 - l_1 \in [0, 1]$. Define countries A and B to share the same cone of diversification if the span of $\left\{\binom{1}{k_1}, \binom{1}{k_2}\right\}$ intersects the span of $\left\{\binom{1}{k'_2}, \binom{1}{k'_2}\right\}$. The set of intersection will itself be a cone of diversification.

It follows from the earlier analysis that if two countries share the same cone of diversification and marginal products across states of nature are spanned by internationally traded securities, factor price equalization will occur. This is stated in Proposition 4.4. Recall, however, that in the general case with internationally traded securities and incomplete markets it is not guaranteed that marginal products will be spanned by the return of traded securities. Two cases where this is guaranteed are the case of complete markets and the special case of multiplicative uncertainty.

PROPOSITION 4.4 *In the model of Proposition 4.2 let J have non-zero determinant for countries A and B and assume that the value of state dependent marginal products for factors for both countries lie in the space spanned by the return of traded securities. Then there exists at least one common cone of diversification. Further if countries A and B share the same cone, factor price equalization obtains and each good is produced using the same production technique across countries.*

Proof Since country A satisfying (4.10) has non-zero det J, the solution to (4.10) is locally unique. Let (k_1, k_2) be the solution. By the full empolyment conditions $l_1 \binom{1}{k_1} + 1 - l_1 \binom{1}{k_2} = \binom{1}{k}$ where $l_1 = L_1/L \in (0, 1)$. Hence there is a cone of diversification containing $\binom{1}{k}$ (generated by variation in l_1). If countries A and B share the same cone of diversification by hypothesis, equalize their capital and labor endowments to the common value k^* such that $\binom{1}{k^*}$ is in the cone of diversification, leaving the individual industry capital labor intensities constant. Both countries' production structures are now identical, satisfying (4.10) and the full employment conditions. Since the value of state dependent marginal products are spanned by the returns of traded securities (4.11) applies and therefore (4.10) is identical for both countries. Local univalence then implies $k_1 = k'_1$, $k_2 = k'_2$. State dependent marginal products are therefore the same across countries. By lemma 4.1 factor price equalization occurs. However, by (4.7) $\hat{w} = \hat{r} = 0$ for the change to k^*, hence factor prices were equal initially. ∎

COROLLARY 4.4 *In the model of Proposition* 4.2 *if countries A and B share the same cone of diversification, the determinant of J is non-zero, and there are complete markets or production uncertainty takes the multiplicative form, then factor price equalization occurs.*

D. The Heckscher–Ohlin Theorem and the pattern of trade

The Heckscher–Ohlin Theorem states that a country will export the commodity whose product is intensive in the use of the country's most abundant factor. There are two definitions of abundance based on relative physical endowments and based on relative autarkic prices of factors. We will consider the quantity version first.

In the deterministic model the quantity version of the theorem requires factor price equalization between countries since factor intensity reversals must be ruled out (to rule out the possibility that a good is capital intensive in the capital abundant country and labor intensive in the labor abundant country requiring both to export the same good for the theorem to hold). In addition, the absence of demand biases is required (to rule out the possibility that home demand for the abundant-factor intensive good does not lead to importing it, e.g., the vineyard-land abundant French demand wine so greatly as to import it.)

The argument in the deterministic case runs as follows. Starting from the initial world trade equilibrium adjust factor endowments between the two countries without changing world production until they are equal except for a scale multiple. This can be done since both countries share a common cone of diversification. Since k_1, k_2, w, r are equal across countries and unchanged by this shift, incomes in the two countries are unchanged as well, and consumption is unchanged at the original price. Identical homothetic demands implies that each country's consumption is identical to its production, with relative scale across countries proportional to relative income. Since prices were constant during the shift in endowments, the Rybczynski Theorem says that the move back to the original position will increase the relative output of the good intensive in the abundant factor of each country. At the original equilibrium, therefore, each country will have an excess supply of the good intensive in its abundant factor. The same argument can be carried over to the model with uncertainty (with one small caveat) provided that factor price equalization is present. We will discuss the caveat shortly. Recognizing that the conditions for factor price equalization are more stringent under conditions of uncertainty, the Heckscher–Ohlin Theorem will fail under conditions that would be sufficient in the deterministic model. The reason for the failure, again, is differences in prices $\beta_j(\alpha)$ across countries and subsequent divergence in the relevant equations (4.10) applying in the two countries. Consequently, we will begin by presuming factor price equalization to hold at the outset. Conditions such as complete markets, or multiplicative production uncertainty which yield factor price equalization are therefore automatically covered as special cases (as in Corollaries 4.3, 4.4).

The caveat to which we now turn our attention has to do with the international pattern of equity ownership. This issue seems to have been totally overlooked in the literature on trade and uncertainty. In the certainty model it is assumed that the value of output accrues as domestic income to home country residents. But factor price equalization under uncertainty, except for chance, requires international trade in equities. If follows that the home country may not own 100% of its domestic firms and vice versa for the foreign country. As a consequence, trade patterns are no longer related solely to home production and income, but also to the pattern of asset ownership. As a simple demonstration return to the income and budget constraint of the investor (assume $\omega_j^i(\alpha) = 0$)

$$\sum_j \bar{\theta}_j^i(P_j - wL_j - rK_j) = \sum_j \theta_j^i P_j + b^i \qquad (4.12)$$

$$I^i(\alpha) = \sum_j \theta_j^i p_j(\alpha) F_j + \rho w L^i + \rho r K^i + \rho b^i. \qquad (4.13)$$

Summing over i (assuming for simplicity that home investors own 100% of domestic stock plus the fraction γ_j of foreign firms $j = 1, 2$) implies

$$\rho w L + \rho r K = \rho b \qquad (4.12')$$

$$\sum_i I^i(\alpha) = p_1(\alpha)y_1(\alpha) + p_2(\alpha)y_2(\alpha) + \gamma_1 p_1(\alpha)y_1'(\alpha)$$
$$+ \gamma_2 p_2(\alpha)y_2'(\alpha) + \rho w L + \rho r K + \rho b, \qquad (4.13')$$

where superscript ' denotes foreign output. Substituting (4.12') into (4.13'), it follows that,

$$p_1(\alpha)x_1(\alpha) + p_2(\alpha)x_2(\alpha) = p_1(\alpha)y_1(\alpha) + p_2(\alpha)y_2(\alpha) + \gamma_1 p_1(\alpha)y_1'(\alpha)$$
$$+ \gamma_2 p_2(\alpha)y_2'(\alpha) \qquad (4.14)$$

where x_1, x_2 represent consumption of goods 1 and 2 by the home country. Thus it is possible that the home country could import *both* goods 1 and 2,

$$p_1(\alpha)E_1(\alpha) + p_2(\alpha)E_2(\alpha) = \gamma_1 p_1(\alpha)y_1'(\alpha) + \gamma_2 p_2(\alpha)y_2'(\alpha) > 0 \qquad (4.15)$$

paying for them from the earnings of its investments abroad. Moreover trade patterns can differ with other patterns of ownership and over different states of nature.

In spite of these problems, the following result can be salvaged of the Heckscher–Ohlin Theorem. Because factor price equalization holds $k_1 = k_1'$, $k_2 = k_2'$ and $y_1'(\alpha) = Ay_1(\alpha)$, $y_1'(\alpha) = By_2(\alpha)$ for some scalars A and B. Using this to re-write (4.14) and (4.15) yields,

$$p_1(\alpha)E_1(\alpha) + p_2(\alpha)E_2(\alpha) = 0 \qquad (4.16)$$

where

$$E_1(\alpha) \equiv x_1(\alpha) - (1 + A\gamma_1)y_1(\alpha)$$
$$E_2(\alpha) \equiv x_2(\alpha) - (1 + B\gamma_e)y_2(\alpha).$$

If $\gamma_1 = \gamma_2 = 0$ this reduces to the usual balanced trade condition in current account. Next choose any of $\beta^i(\alpha)$ $i = 1, \ldots, m$, $\beta_1(\alpha)$, $\beta_2(\alpha)$ to write the average balanced trade condition (in present value terms) as,

$$\sum_\alpha \beta_1(\alpha)p_1(\alpha)E_1(\alpha) + \sum_\alpha \beta_1(\alpha)p_2(\alpha)E_2(\alpha)$$
$$= \sum_\alpha \beta_1(\alpha)[p_1(\alpha)x_1(\alpha) + p_2(\alpha)x_2(\alpha)] - (1 + A\gamma_1)P_1 - 1 + B\gamma_2)P_2$$
$$= 0.$$

This says that the present value of consumption equals, $(1 + A\gamma_1)P_1 + (1 + B\gamma_2)P_2$, the value of the country's asset holdings.[13] The same argument used to prove the Heckscher–Ohlin Theorem in the certainty model now applies under uncertainty for the average direction of trade over states of nature $\sum_\alpha \beta_1(\alpha)E_1(\alpha)$ and $\sum_\alpha \beta_2(\alpha)E_2(\alpha)$ assuming that each country's demands $\sum_\alpha \beta_1(\alpha)x_1(\alpha)$ and $\sum_\alpha \beta_1(\alpha)x_2(\alpha)$ are proportional to the country's share of world wealth.

PROPOSITION 4.5 *In the model of Proposition 4.2 assume that*

(1) *J has non-zero determinant for countries A and B,*
(2) *Countries A and B share a common cone of diversification,*
(3) *The value of state dependent marginal products for factors for both countries lie in the space spanned by the returns of traded securities, and*
(4) *For $\beta(\alpha)$ chosen from the set $\{\beta^i(\alpha), \beta_1(\alpha), \beta_2(\alpha)\}$ $\sum_\alpha \beta(\alpha)p_1(\alpha)x_1(\alpha)$, $\sum_\alpha \beta(\alpha)p_2(\alpha)x_2(\alpha)$ for each country are proportional to the country's share in world wealth.*

---

[13] Because assets are traded all investors agree on the value of $y_1(\alpha)$ and $y_2(\alpha)$, this is why it does not matter which $\beta(\alpha)$ is used to value the output.

Then in present value terms adjusted for world asset ownership the capital abundant country exports the capital intensive good and the labor abundant country exports the labor intensive good. That is, for capital abundant country 1, and capital intensive good 1,

$$\sum_\alpha \beta(\alpha)E_1(\alpha) < 0$$

and for the labor abundant country

$$\sum_\alpha \beta(\alpha)E_2'(\alpha) < 0.$$

Proof By Proposition 4.4 techniques of production are the same across countries,

$$k_1 = k_1'$$
$$k_2 = k_2'$$

By hypothesis 2 both countries share the same cone of diversification. Let x be the percent of world portfolio wealth held by country A measured by prices $\beta(\alpha)$. Transfer endowments between countries such that country A has x percent, and country B has $1-x$ percent. Since both countries have the same cone of diversification, this does not alter prices, incomes or total world production, but now each country produces at home what it consumes. By the Rybczynski Theorem, therefore, a move of endowments back to their original position implies an excess supply of the capital intensive good in the capital abundant country, and an excess supply of the labor intensive good in the labor abundant country. ∎

The price version of the Heckscher–Ohlin Theorem is much less susceptible to generalization than the quantity version. Assuming that the country with the lower relative autarkic price exports the good, the price version compares the autarkic wage-rentals of the two countries. The country with the lower value is said to be labor abundant and is predicted to have the lower relative autarkic price for the labor intensive good. The theorem requires the absence of factor intensity reversals between the countries to guarantee the same monotonic relationship between w/r and the relative autarkic prices of the goods. Essentially the theorem is a statement about the relationship between relative output prices and factor prices in production. Under uncertainty however output is a composite commodity $(F_j(K_j, L_j, 1), \ldots, F_j(K_j, L_j, S))$ with corresponding prices $(\beta_j(1)p_j(1), \ldots, \beta_j(S)p_j(S))$. Trade in the composite commodity is no longer related to prices for the composite commodity in autarky because the two products are different stochastic products. Locally, the generalized Stolper–Samuelson theorem gives a relationship between changes in w, r and prices dP_1', dP_2' (price changes weighted by initial outputs). Moving from the trade position with factor price equalization in the direction of autarky therefore causes prices to move in the required direction relative to w, r but does not provide a global comparison as it does in the certainty case. The reason is that the composite commodity itself changes.

One simple way in which P_1 and P_2 can be made global monotonic functions of w/r is to restrict production to the form

$$y_1(\alpha) = \phi_1(\alpha)h_1(K_1, L_1)$$
$$y_2(\alpha) = \phi_2(\alpha)h_2(K_2, L_2).$$

No matter what choice of K_j, L_j are made y_1 and y_2 will remain the same stochastic product. Then

$$P_j = \sum_\alpha \beta_j(\alpha)p_j(\alpha)\phi_j(\alpha)h_j(K_j, L_j)$$
$$= \Omega_j h_j(K_j, L_j)$$

where Ω_j is the composite price $\sum_\alpha \beta_j(\alpha)p_j(\alpha)\phi_j(\alpha)$. Since the firm's maximization reduces to

$$\underset{K_j, L_j}{\text{Max}}\ \Omega_j h_j(K_j, L_j) - wL_j - rK_j$$

Ω_j and hence P_j becomes a global monotonic function of k_j.[14] If $k_1 - k_2$ is always one-signed for all w/r then k_j is a monotonic function of (w/r) as in the usual model and the result generalizes. The crucial step is restricting the composite commodity to the same stochasic product so that a price for the same product can be identified with the usual relation between prices and output given by the convexity of production sets.

---

[14] Note that Ω_1/Ω_2, h_1/h_2 and $\Omega_1 h_1/\Omega_2 h_2$ all move in the same direction, as in the certainty model, where Ω_j is the usual price of output.

E. The relation between prices and quantities

In the deterministic model of general equilibrium with competitive production an increase in the price of a good leads to an increase in supply. In terms of factors, this implies that an increase in the supply of a factor leads to a reduction in its price.[15] This can be shown by letting $y_0, y_1 \in R^l$ be output and $P_0, P_1 \in R^l$ be prices where subscripts 0 and 1 refer to the initial and final positions. By profit maximization

$$p_1 \cdot y_1 > p_1 \cdot y_0 \qquad (4.17)$$
$$p_0 \cdot y_0 > p_0 \cdot y_1$$

Thus

$$(p_1 - p_0) \cdot (y_1 - y_0) \geq 0. \qquad (4.18)$$

If all prices but component h are unchanged, (4.18) becomes $\Delta p_h \cdot \Delta y_h \geq 0$ which implies that output of good h must increase or remain fixed in response to an increase in its price. If good h is a factor input (entering y as a negative number) then (4.18) implies that an increase in the factor must lead to no change or a decrease in the factor reward. Since (4.18) depends only on profit maximization at the given prices it carries over to the model under uncertainty for prices $\beta_j(\alpha)p_j(\alpha)$ and quantities $F_j(K_j, L_j, \alpha)$ and for factors and factor rewards. This is not true for future spot prices $p_j(\alpha)$ and output as the following example shows.

Consider the model of section A where production satisfies (4.6) and future relative spot prices are given by $p = p_1/p_2$. As discussed there, an increase in p can result in an increase or decrease in k_1, k_2 depending on the economy's demand for the risky asset as wealth rises. Since uncertainty is multiplicative, production is chosen as if the economy were maximizing the value of output $h_1(K_1, L_1)$, $h_2(K_2, L_2)$ at the prices $\sum_\alpha \beta_1(\alpha)p_1\alpha$, $\sum_\alpha \beta_2(\alpha)p_2$, w and r. Figure 4.1 draws the implied contract curve for capital and labor allocations assuming $k_1 - k_2 > 0$.

It is clear that an increase in k_1 and k_2 requires a reduction in output of good 1 in each state and vice versa for a decrease. An increase in p could lead to an increase in k_1, k_2 and hence a

---

[15] In both cases zero responses are also allowed.

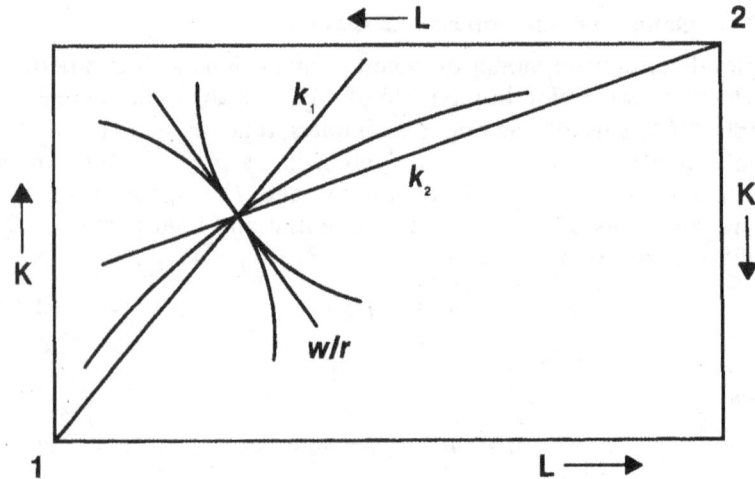

FIGURE 4.1 Contract curve for capital and labor.

reduction in the output of good 1. The reason, of course, is that changes in $\beta_1(\alpha)$, $\beta_2(\alpha)$, reflecting the willingness of investors to hold risk, may move in a direction counter to the primary effect of the increase in p. Thus the effect of spot prices on risk prices must be taken into account.

PROPOSITION 4.6 *In the model of Proposition 4.2 an increase in $\beta_j(\alpha)p_j(\alpha)$, other prices held constant, leads to an increase in output $F_j(K_j, L_j, \alpha)$. A reduction in w (r), other prices held constant, is associated with an increase in the supply of labor (capital).*

Proof Let

$$q = (\beta_1(1)p_1(1), \ldots, \beta_1(S)p_1(S);$$
$$\beta_2(1)p_2(1), \ldots, \beta_2(S)p_2(S); w, r)$$
$$y = (F_1(K_1, L_1, 1), \ldots, F_1(K_1, L_1, S);$$
$$F_2(K_2, L_2, 1), \ldots, F_2(K_2, L_2, S); -L, -k)$$

Since firms maximize the value of output y at prices q,

$$\Delta q \cdot \Delta y \geq 0.$$

This implies that $\Delta\beta_j(\alpha)p_j(\alpha) \cdot \Delta F_j(K_j, L_j, \alpha) \leq 0$ or

$$\Delta w \cdot \Delta L_j \leq 0$$
$$\Delta r \cdot \Delta K_j \leq 0$$

under the conditions of the theorem. ■

We conclude with the following generalization.

PROPOSITION 4.7 *In the model of Proposition 4.2 let $k_1 - k_2 > 0$ (resp. <0). Then an increase in any subset of prices from any of the following sets $\{\beta_1(\alpha)p_1(\alpha)\}$, $\{\beta_1(\alpha)\}$, $\{p_1(\alpha)\}$ with all remaining prices $\beta_j(\alpha)$, $p_j(\alpha)$ constant implies an increase (decrease) in $\Sigma_\alpha \beta_1(\alpha)p_1(\alpha)F_1(K_1, L_1, \alpha)$; $F_1(K_1, L_1, \alpha)$, $\alpha = 1, \ldots, s$; r; $-w$; $-k_1$, and $-k_2$.*

Proof The increase in prices implies $\hat{r} > \hat{P}_1' > \hat{P}_2' = 0 > \hat{w}$ by Proposition 4.1. The increase in r implies that $dk_2 < 0$ by the first order condition for industry 2's use of capital, and the fall in w implies $dk_1 < 0$ by the first order condition for industry 1's use of labor. The full employment condition $l_1 k_1 + (1 - l_1)k_2 = k$ then implies that $dl_1 > 0$. Thus,

$$dP_1 = dP_1' + \sum_\alpha \beta_1(\alpha)p_1(\alpha)dF_1(K_1, L_1, \alpha)$$
$$= dP_1' + \sum_\alpha \beta_1(\alpha)p_1(\alpha)[L(dl_1 + l_1 f_1' dk_1)] > 0$$

since $dP_1' > 0$ and $dl_1, f_1' dk_1 > 0$. Changing $k_1 - k_2 < 0$ reverses the argument by implying $\hat{w} > \hat{P}_1' > \hat{P}_2' = 0 > \hat{r}$. ■

F. Summary

The Stolper–Samuelson Theorem and Rybczynski Theorem generalize to uncertainty when the value of production is used to replace the commodity spot price in the deterministic case. This was proved in terms of two magnification theorems which reduce to the Stolper–Samuelson and Rybczynski theorems as special cases. In one case the value of production is considered as a price-weighted average of output and in another as an output-weighted average of price.

The Heckscher–Ohlin Theorem and Factor Price Equalization Theorem do not generalize except in very special cases. This is essentially due to the fact that risk prices enter into the firm's choice of production. Unless trade in risk markets leads to the same prices in risk worldwide, information about commodity prices is not enough to guarantee identical factor prices or a given pattern of trade.

G. Bibliographic notes

The treatment of the price version of the Heckscher–Ohlin theorem in this section is based on Dumas [1980]. In addition to the already-cited papers, a treatment of theorems of the Stolper–Samuelson type when commodity prices are random may be found in Kemp, Long and Okuguchi [1981].

5. THE GAINS FROM TRADE

The modern treatment of the gains from trade has generally been discussed in terms of two major propositions. The first states that a free trade (world competitive) equilibrium cannot be improved upon by (i.e., is not Pareto superior to) any no-trade (autarkic) equilibrium. The second states that for any autarkic equilibrium there exists a Pareto superior free trade equilibrium. Both propositions are true in an unrestricted Debreu model of general equilibrium, but go further than general competitive theory in several respects. Since the population whose welfare is being considered is a subset of the world population, allowance must be made for this difference. In addition, to prove the benefits of free trade lumpsum transfers are prohibited between countries. This means that the second fundamental theorem of welfare economics which states that any Pareto optimum can be supported as a (world) competitive equilibrium cannot be applied since its proof requires the use of international lumpsum transfers.

But there are other considerations which must also be taken into account. These are particularly important in describing the gains from trade under uncertainty. The measure of welfare improvement must be chosen. The definition of autarky and free trade must be unambiguous, and even the definition of a country must be clear. The internal use of lump sum transfers, which implies that risk-sharing opportunities may be implicitly being used, must be clarified. The source of these concerns is the possibility of foreign ownership of assets and the welfare effect of changing markets structures for spreading risk. The following example will show some of the issues involved.

Consider a country whose capital stock and securities are 100 percent owned by foreigners living within the physical boundaries of the country in question. Domestic residents own only their own labor endowments. Assume that the country initially does not trade with the rest of the world, and that the operating of trade uniformly reduces the relative price of the labor intensive good and hence the real wage. Then the move to free trade is unambiguously welfare harming to the domestic residents. It would seem to imply that free trade is not better than autarky.

Such a conclusion would be false. It would fail because it misunderstands the definitions of a country, autarky, free trade, and the role of foreign ownership. In the initial equilibrium foreigners owned domestic securities, although they lived in the domestic country. Initially there was no foreign trade, in the sense of transport of goods across the home country's physical boundaries. However, autarky is defined as the state in which domestic citizens have *no* economic dealings with foreigners. In the example this is violated in both the securities markets (foreigners own domestic assets) and the goods markets (income from ownership of assets by foreigners must have been spent domestically since no goods crossed the country's boundaries). The welfare result which followed is therefore a demonstration of the fact that a restricted equilibrium can sometimes be welfare improving for a subgroup in the same way that a tariff can improve the welfare of a country over free trade. It does not compare autarky to free trade.

The notion of a country as a physical location is inadequate once foreign ownership of assets and migration of factors and citizens of different nationalities is allowed. We will adhere to the definition of a country given in Chapter 1 which avoids this problem. A country is a specified collection of individuals, their endowments, and firms, regardless of the physical locations they may retire to. Autarky is the state defined by no economic transactions between residents of different countries. In particular, this implies no trade in commodities (goods or services) including the hiring of foreign factors of production and no foreign ownership of securities or firm shares. Free trade is taken to mean the unrestricted international trade of goods and services as well as trade in securities markets.

Given the proper definitions for country, autarky and free trade under uncertainty are there still necessarily gains from trade? The answer depends on the structure of the markets for sharing risk. If these are complete, the traditional conclusions hold. If they are incomplete, or absent, the traditional conclusions need not hold. The explanation for this is that the model of world general equilibrium under uncertainty with complete markets is formally identical to a deterministic model of world equilibrium with redefined goods. The jointness of the production structure which uncertainty imparts does not play a role in the gains from trade propositions. They, therefore, apply without modification from the deterministic case.

When markets are incomplete things are more complicated. In particular, competitive general equilibrium with incomplete markets need not be Pareto optimal. Pareto superior allocations may exist, and some of these can be autarkic equilibria. An example will be given in Part B. The main message from this is that there are two types of welfare effects which follow from the move to free trade. The first is the traditional gain from trade in spot markets, the second is the gain or loss from trade in risk markets. If the welfare effect of free trade on the ability of domestic investors to risk-spread should be negative, and larger than the effects of free trade in spot markets, the opening of trade can have harmful welfare consequences. In Part A below we will show that free trade, with complete markets, can only be welfare improving. (The general treatment of the gains from trade in a deterministic setting can be found in Kemp and Wan [1987].) Part B considers the case of incomplete markets with a counter-example showing the possibility of risk market losses greater than direct effects (this will be considered again in Chapter 7 when commerical policy is discussed). Part C discusses the nature of optimality in models with incomplete risk markets.

A. The gains from trade under uncertainty with complete security markets

To prove the first proposition, that a free trade equilibrium cannot be improved upon by any autarkic equilibrium, we take a home country point of view. The method of proof is quite general, relying on the properties of convex sets and separating hyperplanes. For simplicity, consider first the case of world competitive equilibrium in a deterministic Debreu model. Let home country aggregate consumption be $x^* \in R^l$, home production $(y^* + \omega) \in R^l$, and equilibrium prices p^*. Then $p^* \cdot x^* = p^* \cdot (y^* + \omega) + F^*$ where F^* is net income from ownership of foreign assets.[16] The set of all outputs having the property that some distribution of them to home consumers would leave no consumer worse off than at the original equilibrium is a convex set.[17] Call this set V. By revealed preference, any point in V has strictly greater value than x^*, $p^* \cdot v > p^* \cdot x^*$ for $v \in V$.[18] Similarily, by profit maximization $p^* \cdot y^* \geq p^* \cdot y$ for any other feasible choice of production y. In autarky $F^* = 0$. It follows that if $F^* \geq 0$, no point in the feasible autarkic production set Y is also contained in V. Thus no autarkic equilibrium can improve on free trade if $F^* \geq 0$. The logic is shown in Figure 5.1.

Initial production is y^* on the frontier of the feasible production set $\{\omega\} + Y$, shown as set $0Ay^*B$. Consumption is at point x^* with the preferred set given by V. Prices p^* are indicated in the slopes of lines l_1 and l_2. Net foreign ownership income is given by the distance F^*. Since V and $\{\omega\} + Y$ are convex sets separated by hyperplanes l_1 or l_2 no point in $\{\omega\} + Y$ (autarky) can also be a member of V (improve on x^*). To translate the argument to trade with uncertainty and complete markets replace the prices of the form p_h with prices of the type $\beta(\alpha)p_j(\alpha)$ where $\beta(\alpha)$ is the price of a pure elementary security and $p_j(\alpha)$ is the future spot price of the

---

[16] F^* must be included since the initial equilibrium may entail foreign ownership of stock shares. For example, if half of home production output is owned by foreign nationals and half of foreign output y' is owned domestically, then $F^* = p^* \cdot (y' - y^*)/2$.

[17] This is the familiar Scitovsky construction.

[18] If v has lesser or equal value at least one consumer could purchase a preferred or indifferent bundle at existing prices and incomes, holding other consumers constant, contradicting the fact that x^* is preferred.

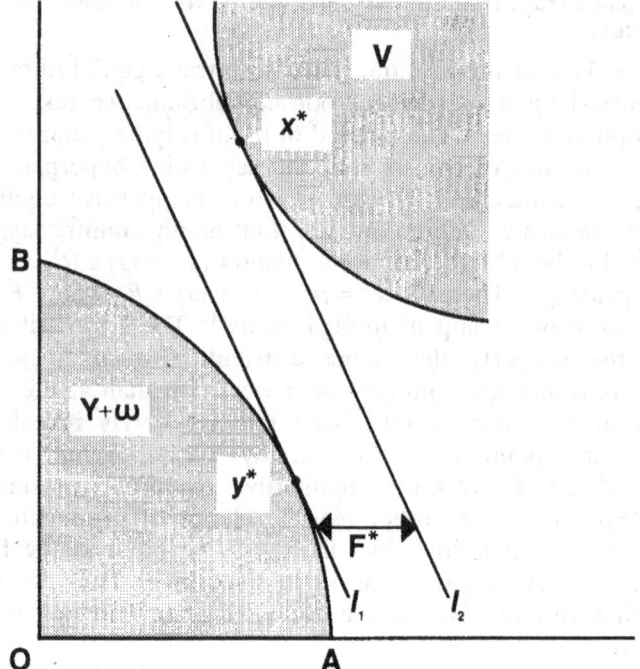

FIGURE 5.1 Autarkic welfare relative to free trade.

commodity in state α. $p^* \cdot y^*$ then becomes the present market value of output and F^* the net value of security holdings.

PROPOSITION 5.1 *Let $\mathscr{E}$ be a world free trade equilibrium under uncertainty with complete security markets, and let F_k be the value of net foreign security holdings of country k evaluated at equilibrium prices $\{\beta(\alpha)p_j(\alpha)\}$. If $F_k \geq 0$ then no autarkic allocation for country k can be Pareto superior to its allocation in $\mathscr{E}$.*

A simple extension of Proposition 5.1 follows in the case where there is a single consumer even if markets are incomplete. The extension requires only that domestic firms maximize the value of output in terms of the consumer's prices. The generalization does not apply to multiple consumers unless internal risk sharing is such as to equalize consumers' subject prices for risk. With one consumer this condition is automatically satisfied since risk-sharing is effectively perfect internally by default. The argument runs as follows. Let p^i represent the vector of prices with individual elements of the form $\beta^i(\alpha)p_j(\alpha)$, and let x^i represent the conformable vector of the individual's consumption of goods over states of nature. By construction of the prices p^i and convexity of preferences a preferred consumption has a value at prices p^i greater than $p^i \cdot x^i$. The value of consumption in state α at prices $p_j(\alpha)$ is given by $I^i(\alpha)$, the individual's income in that state. Thus for consumption $\hat{x}^i$ to be in the preferred set requires $\sum_i p^i \hat{x}^i \geq \sum_i \beta^i(\alpha)I^i(\alpha)$. But $\sum_i \beta^i(\alpha)I^i(\alpha)$ is maximized by the choice of production of country k given the net value of country k's ownership of foreign assets F_k valued at $\beta^i(\alpha)$.[19] Thus if $F_k \geq 0$ the better-than set and the set of feasible autarkic productions are separated by a hyperplane. No autarkic equilibrium can improve on free trade.

PROPOSITION 5.2 *Let $\mathscr{E}$ be a world free trade equilibrium under uncertainty with incomplete security markets. Let F_k be the value of net foreign security holdings of country k evaluated at the single set of prices $\{\beta^i(\alpha)p^j(\alpha)\}$. If $F_k \geq 0$ and production in country k maximizes the value of output at prices $\beta^i(\alpha)p_j(\alpha)$ then no autarkic allocation for country k can be Pareto superior to its allocation in $\mathscr{E}$.*

Notice that the absence of international trade in equities guarantees that domestic firms will maximize the value of output at prices $\beta^i(\alpha)p_j(\alpha)$. This is because the only owners of the firm will be domestic. The theorem also applies when there is international trade in equities. However, because foreign owners may have different risk prices it must be checked to see that the firm's choices satisfy the maximization requirement at prices $\beta^i(\alpha)p_j(\alpha)$. One special case in which this is guaranteed is when production uncertainty is multiplicative. In that case the firm's output, no matter what production it chooses, is always the same stochastic product. Since it has the same value to foreign and domestic shareholders (being internationally traded), the firm's choice will maximize its output value in terms of the domestic prices. It is easy

---

[19] By the spanning assumption F_k has the same value whether valued at $\beta^i(\alpha)$ or $\beta^h(\alpha)$ for some other choice of h.

to show that the following corollary, originally proved diagrammatically in the two-good case by Helpman and Razin, need not hold if there is more than one consumer or production uncertainty is not multiplicative.

COROLLARY 5.3 *The conditions of Proposition 5.2 are satisfied if shares to firms are traded internationally and production uncertainty is multiplicative.*

In the one-consumer case or, what is the same thing, the multi-consumer case with perfect intra-country risk-sharing and internal lump sum transfers, the proof that autarky cannot Pareto-dominate free trade is equivalent to the statement that a free trade equilibrium will Pareto dominate autarky. This is because a single consumer cannot be compelled to trade to his own harm. The multi-consumer case is more subtle. To prove that any autarkic equilibrium in the multi-consumer case can be improved upon by free trade (Pareto-wise) requires an existence proof for a world trade equilibrium where each consumer is better off. If markets are complete any world Pareto Optimum can be achieved as a free trade equilibrium since the world is equivalent to a deterministic Debreu general equilibrium model. Since the initial autarkic equilibrium was not a Pareto optimum subsidies can be chosen in such a way that every individual is better off in the free trade equilibrium. The only real issue is whether this can be done without the use of cross country transfers—that is, with each country redistributing income generated by its home production only. In general, the answer to this question would be no, but in the case at hand we have specified that the initial position of country k was autarkic. This will allow us to generate internally the needed transfers.

The essence of the construction is quite simple. Again, consider the deterministic model with autarkic prices p_0, consumption x^i, and aggregate production $y + \omega$ for country k. For individual i to purchase his autarkic bundle x^i at price p his income must satisfy $I^i \geq p \cdot x^i$. For the country as a whole this implies $\sum_i I^i \geq p \cdot x$. But the income of country k in the new equilibrium will be given by $p \cdot (y + \omega) + T$ where T is the cross country transfer, if any. Since $y + \omega = x$ initially in autarky, the income requirement is satisfied for $T \geq 0$. Thus, for the country as a whole to generate enough income for welfare improvement in the new equilibrium no cross country transfers are needed. Retracing the argument, we see that the result follows because trade was initially zero ($x - y - \omega = 0$), and that it applies to *any* potential equilibrium and its associated prices p. Thus if the country simply distributes claims to income derived from home production to households so that each can buy its autarkic bundle if desired, the existence of a free trade equilibrium is equivalent to welfare improvement for country k, individual by individual. Procedures for proving the existence of equilibrium follow from the general equilibrium literature virtually without modification. Adjustment of initial endowments of households using the resources of the home country only, insure the needed income for each consumer. Examples are given in the bibliographic references. The translation to the model with complete securities markets is immediate upon re-interpretation of the model as a deterministic general equilibrium model.

The relationship between the one-consumer case, complete markets and unrestricted internal lump sum transfers should be stressed. As has been noted, unrestricted internal lump sum transfers imply perfect risk-sharing internally. Both are effectively equivalent to the assumption of a single consumer. It is an open question for a multi-consumer economy with imperfect risk markets what type of restrictions can be placed on internal lump sum transfers and still allow any autarkic equilibrium to be Pareto dominated by a free trade equilibrium.[20] Unrestricted transfers guarantee this result, the total prohibition of transfers leads to a failure of this theorem.[21]

B. The gains from trade under uncertainty with multiple consumers and without complete security markets

The tension between changes in risk-sharing capability and gains from trade in spot markets does not exist when markets are complete (or all risk is limited to a subspace for which risk markets exist) because risk spreading is available for all types of risk which

---

[20] A natural restriction is that transfers must take place in claims which already exist in the available risk markets.

[21] In the deterministic model trade may harm some household or factor relative to autarky. In the absence of transfers free trade is generally Pareto non-comparable to autarky.

are generated by the model. As the sophistication of the risk markets declines, however, we would expect to find one type of gain outweighed by losses of another type in the move to free trade. This is precisely what we find. The following example presents a situation in which risk markets are imperfect after the opening of free trade but were perfect to a greater or lesser extent in autarky depending on parameters of risk aversion. Consequently, neither the free trade equilibrium nor the autarkic equilibrium need be a Pareto optimum. Either could Pareto dominate the other.[22]

Imagine two identical regions which grow a risky crop and a safe crop. In the absence of trade, price rises for the risky crop whenever output falls. Consumers allocated their non-random income between the two goods. Assume that consumer demand has unitary price elasticity so that total farm income is constant. All the risk is therefore borne by consumers who are assumed to be risk neutral. Now let trade open up and assume that total output of the risky crop is constant between the two countries (perfectly negatively correlated). Farmers now face income uncertainty since the price of the risky crop is stabilized but its quantity is not. As farmers shift into greater production of the riskless crop to avoid risk this raises the average price of the risky crop. Since consumers have unit price elasticity (spend a constant amount on both crops) average farm income remains constant, but its variance increases. Thus risk averse farmers suffer welfare losses. Consumers, on the other hand are risk neutral, but face higher prices for the risky crop. This rise in price can make consumers worse off, showing that the move to free trade was welfare harming. By proper choice of parameters the free trade equilibrium can be made unique. Thus the example shows welfare losses from the move to free trade: a free trade equilibrium was constructed which was Pareto inferior to autarky.[23]

The explanation is fairly straightforward. In the original equilibrium risk averse farmers held no risk while risk neutral consumers bore all risk. The specific functional forms happened to efficiently share risk even through no formal markets for risk

---

[22] The example is drawn from Newbery and Stiglitz [1984].

[23] Consumers can also be made risk averse if desired. For a detailed treatment see Newbery and Stiglitz, *op. cit.*

existed. When trade opened up, however, the absence of formal risk markets meant that risk need not be optimally distributed in the new situation. In the extreme circumstances of the example, all risk after trade is open is held by risk averse farmers and no risk is held by the risk neutral consumers. The consequent loss in welfare from the misallocation of risk-bearing due to the absence of complete markets leads to an overall welfare loss from the opening of trade.

C. Optimality of world free trade

The failure of free trade to Pareto dominate autarky in the absence of international trade in securities and complete markets follows essentially from the failure of the free trade equilibrium to achieve Pareto optimality. The comparison then becomes one between one sub-optimal equilibrium and another. The set of Pareto optimal allocations have the property that no allocation in the set is dominated by another. This is not true for incomplete market equilibria.

The industrial organization literature and finance literature has spent a great deal of time describing the optimality properties for the incomplete markets equilibria of the type discussed here. The

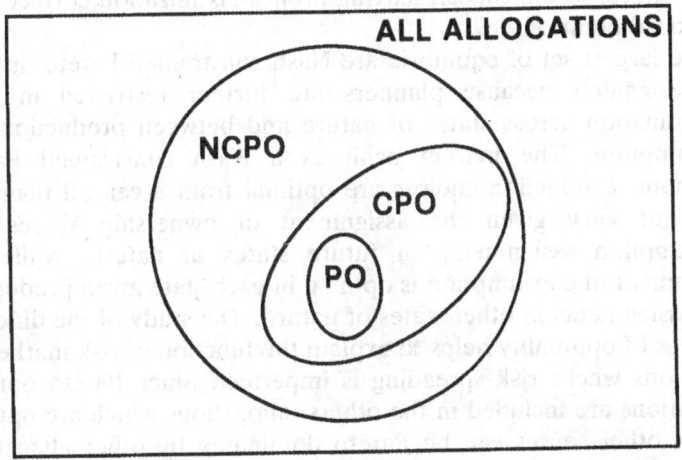

FIGURE 5.2 Nesting of degrees of market optimality.

results can be summarized by the use of Figure 5.2. In Figure 5.2 a Venn diagram is drawn showing the relationship between all allocations and three types of optimal allocations. The smallest set of allocations is the set of Pareto optimal allocations. Stock market equilibria with complete markets are in this set. The next largest set of allocations are constrained Pareto optimal allocations, so designated because they represent the set of all allocations which could be achieved by a central planner who was constrained in his allocations to those which could be achieved through the restrictions imposed by stock market share ownership. That is, only allocations which can be achieved through reassignment of initial wealth, share ownership and firm production choices are allowed. In a one good model, or if markets are not allowed to re-open for spot trading after each state of nature is revealed, the stock market achieves a constrained Pareto optimum. However, if multiple goods are present (as in the models discussed here) and markets re-open, the market generally does not achieve a constrained Pareto optimum (see the references cited in the bibliographic notes). The reason is that firms treat future prices $p_j(\alpha)$ as given and only consider the welfare effect of their production choices on investor welfare through income effects ($I^i(\alpha)$) while the central planner considers the effect of changing prices $p_j(\alpha)$. If markets were complete, the price effects would cancel, leaving profit maximization correct from the social point of view.

The largest set of equilibria are Nash constrained Pareto optima, so designated because planners are further restricted in their co-ordination across states of nature and between production and consumption. The market achieves a Nash constrained Pareto optimum. Production choices are optimal from a central planner's point of view given the assignment of ownership shares and consumption assignments in future states of nature, while the assignment of consumption is optimal in each state given production and assignments in other states of nature. The study of the different degrees of optimality helps to explain the function of risk markets in situations where risk spreading is imperfect. Since Pareto optimal allocations are included in the others, allocations which are optimal in the other senses can be Pareto dominated by other allocations within the same set. Examples are available in the literature.

D. Summary

The study of gains from trade under uncertainty is a difficult topic because there is no natural metric for measuring the degree of imperfection due to imperfect risk sharing. Generally speaking, when markets are complete, all of the traditional gains from trade conclusions carry over to the uncertainty case, but when markets for risk are incomplete they generally do not.

Results of the traditional gains from trade type are available for a one consumers economy, but these follow only because risk sharing is internally perfect by default when there is only one consumer. When multiple consumers are present domestically the move to free trade may have the unintended effect of reducing risk sharing opportunities. Losses from greater inefficiency in risk sharing can outweight traditional gains from trade, leading to an overall loss. An example of this type was presented. A discussion of the marginal measurement of the two types of welfare effects is given in Chapter 7.

E. Bibliographic notes

Papers in the industrial organization and finance literature dealing with the optimality properties of general equilibrium under uncertainty with incomplete markets include Diamond [1967], Drèze [1974], Stiglitz [1982], Grinols [1985b] and the references cited by them. References dealing specifically with gains from trade under uncertainty include Newbery and Stiglitz [1984], Fries [1983, 1984], Kemp and Ohyama [1978] and Helpman and Razin [1978]. Grandmont and McFadden [1972] and Kemp and Wan [1972] definitively discuss the Pareto superiority of free trade relative to autarky in the absence of uncertainty. Kemp and Wan [1987] provide a comprehensive treatment of the gains from trade in the deterministic model.

6. TARIFFS AND QUOTAS

One of the most interesting issues in uncertainty and the theory of international trade is the extent to which traditional commerical policy conclusions can be applied in the new framework. If the ultimate purpose of economics is to understand and improve the economy's generation of welfare, then the ultimate purpose for trade theory should be improvement in the understanding and use of commerical policy. We have taken one step in this direction already in the previous chapter's discussion of the gains from trade. In this chapter we begin a formal discussion of commerical policy. However, because of the particular importance of tariffs in the traditional literature, and to a lesser extent quotas, we devote this chapter to several issues peculiar to tariffs and quotas and continue in the following chapter with a more general discussion of commercial policy.

A number of topics and and propositions have traditionally been associated with the study of tariffs. Among the important issues which we will discuss in this chapter are the protective effects of a tariff, the symmetry between export and import taxes, and the ranking of tariffs versus quotas. The question of the calculation of the optimal tariff will be postponed to Chapter 7. In most respects, the usual results of tariff theory carry over to the uncertain environment even when markets are incomplete. In general, new elements and divergences, where they appear, derive from the added effects of the policy on the risk-spreading capabilities of the economy or on the different nature of the tools being studied. The type of tariff depends, for example, on whether one considers a tariff to be state-dependent or state-independent. A similar argument applies to quotas.

A. The protective effect of a tariff

In a deterministic world, the protective effect of a tariff is determined by the effect of the tariff on increasing the price of output for the protected industry. If the relative price of output rises for the industry, production also increases. In the model under uncertainty this simple relation is changed for two reasons. First, output varies from state to state. A change which increases output in one state could lower it in another. Thus the measure of protection must be modified to take into account random output. Second, spot prices $p_j(\alpha)$ are no longer sufficient to determine the allocation of resources. A knowledge of risk prices $\beta_1(\alpha)$, $\beta_2(\alpha)$ are also needed to determine firm demands for resources.

In the two good model the expected effect of a tariff is to raise the relative domestic price of the protected good. Even in the deterministic model, however, it is possible that a tariff could lower the domestic relative price of the protected good due to a large enough drop in the world price for the good.[24] This possibility is ruled out if the country is small in the sense that its choices do not affect world prices for the two goods. Under uncertainty this result will be modified.

To resolve the issue of multiple spot prices, measure the effect of the tariff on prices and output using the relative market values P_2/P_1 where

$$P_1 = \sum_\alpha \beta_1(\alpha) P_1(\alpha) F_1(K_1, L_1, \alpha)$$

$$P_2 = \sum_\alpha \beta_2(\alpha)(1+t) P_2(\alpha) F_2(K_2, L_2, \alpha),$$

good 2 is the protected good and t is the tariff rate. Since price, value, and output move in the same direction in the deterministic model this is a generalization of the usual measure of protection based on value. Notice that for fixed outputs F_1, F_2, P_1 and P_2 become Laspeyres indexes of price and for fixed prices they are Laspeyres indexes of output. A drop in P_2/P_1 would correspond to the paradoxical outcome discussed above for the deterministic model.

Under uncertainty, account must be taken of the size of the country with respect to *two* markets: spot markets and risk markets. Accordingly, we will speak of a country as small relative to spot markets if world prices $p_j(\alpha)$ are invariant with respect to its production and consumption choices. A country is small with respect to risk markets if risk prices $\beta_j(\alpha)$ are invariant with respect to its production and consumption choices.

It is easy to show that a country's "largeness" or "smallness" with respect to one market need not influence its size with respect to another. An example of a country which is large in spot markets but small in risk markets is Puerto Rico. Although it is financially

---

[24] Lerner and Metzler made note of this possibility.

integrated into the United States it accounts for more than 4/5 of all the rum consumed in the United States. In terms of the rum spot market it is large. In terms of financial markets, however, the relative size of Puerto Rico to the United States makes it unlikely that its actions will affect the pricing of risk in the United States. At the other extreme, a country which is a price-taker on world commodity (spot) markets, but is closed to international risk markets, will be unable to influence spot prices. It will nevertheless determine its risk prices internally. It is simultaneously large in risk markets but small in spot markets. Adding the possibilities that a country could be large in both markets, or small in both brings the total to four possible cases.

We first show with uncertainty that a tariff need not lead to an increase in the relative value of output of the protected industry even when all future spot prices for that industry increase. The reason is that risk prices $\beta_j(\alpha)$ may move in the opposite direction leading to a reduction in both output and value of the protected industry.[25] Let utility be given by

$$U = \sum_\alpha \pi_\alpha \log(C_2(\alpha) + \log C_1(\alpha))$$

in a one-comsumer country where production takes the form

$$y_1(\alpha) = \phi_1(\alpha)h_1(K_1, L_1), \quad \phi_1(\alpha) > 1$$
$$y_2(\alpha) = \phi_2(\alpha)h_2(K_2, L_2), \quad \phi_2(\alpha) = 1$$
$$K_1 + K_2 = K, \quad L_1 + L_2 = L.$$

Assume in the initial equilibrium that the country is small in commodity markets and large in risk markets by allowing spot trade in commodities at fixed prices $p_j(\alpha) = 1$ but no international trade in securities. Further, assume initially that $h_1(K_1, L_1) = h_2(K_2, L_2) = 1$. Within the country 100 per cent ownership of firm 2 (resp. firm 1) entitles the holder to a security with certain return 1

---

[25] Actually we have already seen an example of this type in Chapter 4 if we re-interpret the model of Batra [1975] in which production uncertainty is multiplicative in one industry and future spot prices are certain. An increase in the relative spot price of the risky good was shown to lead either to an increase or decrease in its output. Further, since production uncertainty was multiplicative an increase in output in one state of nature corresponds to an increase in all states and vice versa for a decrease.

UNCERTAINTY AND THEORY OF INTERNATIONAL TRADE 65

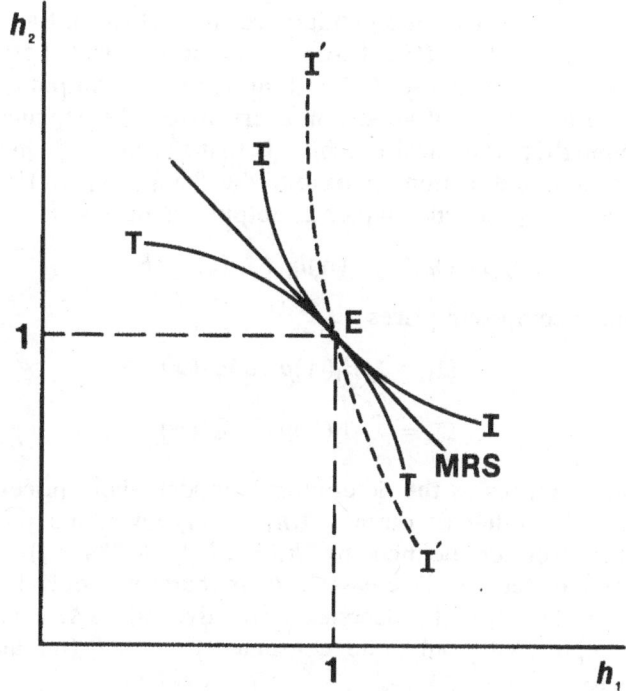

FIGURE 6.1 Equilibrium in security market.

(uncertainty return $\phi_1(\alpha)$) in each state of nature. Since returns are fixed given prices $p_j(\alpha)$ we can plot the initial equilibrium as in Figure 6.1. In each state of nature the consumer takes his income $1 + \phi_1(\alpha)$ and spends it on goods 1 and 2 at world prices $p_j(\alpha)$. Under the assumptions he imports good 2 in each state. Since the investor has chosen his portfolio holdings of firms 1 and 2 to maximize his utility given the supply of the two types of assets we know that equilibrium is at a point such as E where the indifference curve II in security space is tangent to the frontier TT showing maximal output of h_2 given h_1. The marginal rate of substitution between the two types of assets is indicated in the slope of the line labeled MRS.

Now we assume that a tariff is levied on good 2 with revenues disposed of by the government. The effect of the increase in $p_2(\alpha)$

relative to $p_1(\alpha)$ causes the indifference curve II to shift at E in the direction indicated by $I'I'$. The new equilibrium will therefore be at a point to the southeast of E, indicating reduced output of good 2 and increased output of good 1 in every state. The explanation for this seemingly paradoxical outcome is that the prices $\beta_1(\alpha)$, $\beta_2(\alpha)$ have moved in a direction opposite to the change in $p_2(\alpha)/p_1(\alpha)$. In this model, as shown in Chapter 2, output maximizes,

$$\sum \beta_j(\alpha)p_j(\alpha)\phi_j(\alpha)h_j(K_j, L_j) - rK_j - wL_j.$$

By defining composite prices

$$\Omega_1 = \sum_\alpha \beta_1(\alpha)p_1(\alpha)\phi_1(\alpha)$$
$$\Omega_2 = \sum_\alpha \beta_2(\alpha)p_2(\alpha)\phi_2(\alpha) \qquad (6.1)$$

the model reduces to the deterministic model where prices Ω_1, Ω_2 maximize the value of output $\Omega_1 h_1 + \Omega_2 h_2$ given the production possibility frontier defined by $h_1(K_1, L_1)$, $h_2(K_2, L_2)$ and the availability of factors. Decrease in h_2 is therefore equivalent to an decrease in Ω_2/Ω_1 and a decrease in relative values $\Omega_2 h_2/\Omega_1 h_1$. In this example, with only one consumer $\beta_1(\alpha) = \beta_2(\alpha)$ and (6.1) reduces to

$$\Omega_1 = \sum_\alpha \beta_1(\alpha)$$
$$\Omega_2 = \sum_\alpha \beta_1(\alpha)(1+t)\phi_2(\alpha) \qquad (6.2)$$

where t is the tariff rate. In order for Ω_2/Ω_1 to fall with an increase in t it must be that $\sum_\alpha \dfrac{\beta_1(\alpha)}{\sum_\alpha \beta_1(\alpha)} \phi_2(\alpha)$ declines indicating that $\beta_1(\alpha)$ has changed to place relatively greater emphasis on income in states where output of the risky good is low. We summarize in the following proposition.

PROPOSITION 6.1 *If a country is large in risk markets but small in spot markets, an increase in the relative future spot price of a commodity through tariff protection need not lead to an increase in the value of output in the protected industry or its quantity in future states of nature.*

The above analysis suggests that if we add the requirement of smallness in risk markets to the requirement of smallness in spot markets protection always raises the value of output of the protected industry. Proposition 6.2 states this formally. The proof follows directly from application of Proposition 4.7.

PROPOSITION 6.2 *If a country is small with respect to risk markets and spot markets, then a tariff raises the value of output of the protected good, its domestic price in each future state, and its output in each future state.*

In the remaining two cases where a country is large in spot markets, it is clear that paradoxical outcomes are possible through the possibility that the future spot price of the protected good could fall domestically. If this is ruled out, then a paradoxical outcome is impossible if the country is small in risk markets.

B. The symmetry of export and import taxes

Early in the analysis of tariffs in the 2 good case it was noticed that export taxes and tariffs (import taxes) levied at the same rate had the same effect on economy. This symmetry is usually referred to as Lerner symmetry after A. Lerner who first pointed it out. Lerner symmetry is really a property of homogeneous of degree zero demand and supply functions and as such generalizes to multi-commodity general equilibrium models of trade. It follows immediately that it also generalizes to trade under uncertainty when markets are complete. In this section we consider whether it can be extended to incomplete markets with foreign ownership of assets and to tariffs which are set *ex ante*, before the state of nature is revealed. These tariffs effectively apply to a *set* of goods which are imports of a given commodity in different states of nature. We will find that in some cases the proposition does not apply in the hoped for manner.

We will begin with a simple demonstration of Lerner symmetry in the deterministic case and then proceed to the generalizations.

In the deterministic trade model write,

$$x(q, I) = y(q) + \omega + z(p) \qquad (6.3a)$$

$$q = p + t \qquad (6.3b)$$

$$I = q \cdot (y + \omega) + t \cdot z \qquad (6.3c)$$

$$p \cdot z = 0 \qquad (6.3d)$$

(6.3d) defines the trade vector z, (6.3b) defines the tariff t as the difference between world prices p and domestic prices q. Income is given as the value of domestic production plus tariff revenues. (6.3d) is the balance of trade identity. The following proposition generalizes the notion of Lerner symmetry to the system (6.3).

PROPOSITION 6.3 (Lerner Symmetry) *If prices (q, p) are an equilibrium for the system (6.3) with tariff $t = q - p$ then $(\mu q, p)$ is also an equilibrium for the same quantities for the tariff $t = \mu q - p$, and scalar $\mu > 0$.*

Proof In the system (6.3) substitute (d) into (c) to get $I = q \cdot (y + \omega) + (p + t) \cdot z$. Replace $p + t$ by q and substitute into (a) to get

$$x(q, q \cdot (y + \omega + z)) = y(q) + \omega + z(p). \quad (*)$$

Replacing q by μq in (*) leaves the equation unchanged since $y(\mu q) = y(q)$ by homogeneity of degree zero of production and $x(\mu q, \mu q \cdot (y + \omega + z))$ is unchanged by homogeneity of demand of degree zero in prices and income. Direct computation shows (b)—(d) are also satisfied. ∎

As an example of Proposition 6.3 consider the 2 good system with prices

$$p = \begin{pmatrix} 1 \\ 1 \end{pmatrix}, \quad q = \begin{pmatrix} 2 \\ 1 \end{pmatrix}, \quad t = \begin{pmatrix} 1 \\ 0 \end{pmatrix}.$$

Choosing $\mu = 1/2$ this tariff on good 1 is equivalent to an export tax on good 2 where

$$p = \begin{pmatrix} 1 \\ 1 \end{pmatrix}, \quad q = \begin{pmatrix} 1 \\ 1/2 \end{pmatrix} \quad \text{and} \quad t = \begin{pmatrix} 0 \\ -1/2 \end{pmatrix}.$$

In the first case the tax on imports of good 1 is 100% of world price with good 2 untaxed. In the equivalent case the tax on exports of good 2 is 100% of the domestic price with good 1 untaxed.

Proposition 6.3 continues to hold for an open economy under uncertainty with complete markets where prices q are replaced by vectors of the equivalent form $(\beta(\alpha)q_j(\alpha))$ and income is interpreted to mean portfolio wealth. A more interesting question, however, is how the proposition fares when foreign ownership of assets is introduced and markets are incomplete.

To analyze this question, return to the model of Chapter 2. The relevent information is reproduced in the equations below.

$$\sum_i x^i = \sum_j y_j + z \qquad (6.4a)$$

$$x^i(\alpha) = x^i((q_j(\alpha)), I^i(\alpha))$$
$$y_j = y_j(\beta_j(\alpha)q_j(\alpha), w, r) \qquad (6.4b)$$
$$q_j(\alpha) = p_j(\alpha) + t_j(\alpha)$$

$$I^i(\alpha) = \sum q_j(\alpha)F_j(K_j, L_j) + \rho w L^i + \rho r K^i + \rho b^i + F^i(\alpha) + T^i(\alpha)$$
$$(6.4c)$$

$$q(\alpha) \cdot z^i(\alpha) = F^i(\alpha) + T^i(\alpha). \qquad (6.4d)$$

The changes are that consumption is now determined in each state by prices and income in that state and that the individual receives his income from sales of factor services at home plus income from his ownership of domestic and foreign assets. $F^i(\alpha)$ is individual i's net foreign ownership income including international borrowing and lending for the state α, and $T^i(\alpha)$ is his share of tariff revenues in state α. $F^i(\alpha) + T^i(\alpha)$ pay for any trade imbalances $q(\alpha) \cdot z(\alpha)$ measured in domestic prices. The following proposition generalizes Lerner Symmetry to the model of (6.4).

PROPOSITION 6.4 (Lerner Symmetry Under Uncertainty with Foreign Ownership of Assets and Incomplete Markets) *If* $\{[(\beta_j(\alpha)), (q_j(\alpha)), w, r, \rho], [(\beta_j^*(\alpha)), (p_j(\alpha)), w^*, r^*, \rho]\}$ *is an equilibrium price system for the system (6.4) in the model of Chapter 2, where* $[(\beta_j^*(\alpha)), (p_j(\alpha)), w^*, r^*, \rho]$ *are foreign prices, then so are prices,* $\{[(\beta_j(\alpha)), (\mu q_j(\alpha)), \mu w, \mu r, \rho], [(\beta_j^*(\alpha)), (p_j(\alpha)), w^*, r^*, \rho]\}$ *for the same quantities.*

Comment Notice the necessary distinction between spot prices $(q_j(\alpha), p_j(\alpha))$ to which the tariff is applied and the prices in the financial markets $(\beta_j(\alpha), \beta_j^*(\alpha), \rho)$.

Proof From the pricing relation for domestic securities under the new price system $\mu P_j = \sum \beta_j(\alpha)(\mu q_j(\alpha))F_j(K_j, L_j, \alpha)$. From the firm's profit maximization,

$$\sum_\alpha \beta_j(\alpha)[\mu q_j(\alpha)] \frac{\partial F_j}{\partial K_j} = \mu r$$

$$\sum_\alpha \beta_j(\alpha)[\mu q_j(\alpha)] \frac{\partial F_j}{\partial L_j} = \mu w.$$

Hence by the budget constraint

$$\sum_j \bar{\theta}_j^i(\mu P_j - \mu w L_j - \mu r K_j) = \sum_j \theta_j^i \mu P_j + \mu b^i$$

the nominal value of bondholdings rises by μ. Substituting from (6.5d) into (6.4c) income in the new situation rises to $\mu I^i(\alpha)$. Thus domestic prices and income rise by the common proportion μ implying no changes in demands or supplies given choices by the rest of the world $z(\alpha)$. Direct check then shows that the system (6.4) remains in equilibrium with no change in any real variables. $\{(\theta_j^i), (K_j, L_j), (K^i, L^i), (x^i), (y_j)\}$ foreign or domestic. ∎

The system remains in equilibrium even with foreign holdings of assets because the returns to ownership are, in effect, used in the country of generation at local prices to pay for surpluses or deficits in current account trade.

The concept of a tariff which emerges from the above exercise is one which is a state dependent tax on the import of a given commodity. That is, a commodity in each state of nature is theoretically treated above as a separate, distinguishable commodity. Conceptually this is correct, but common usage with uncertain future states treats a tariff as if it were fixed *ex ante* before the state of nature is known and applied at the same rate to the entire set of prices of the given commodity over states of nature. Is it true that such an *ex ante*, state-independent tariff applied as it is to a composite bundle of goods can be set to zero and replaced by an appropriate state independent tariff on the other good?

If the tariff is defined in *ad valorem* form the answer is yes. Otherwise the answer is no. Assume that good 2 is the import good and the presence of an *ad valorem* tariff causes $q_2(\alpha)/p_2(\alpha) = c$ where c is a constant. There is no tariff or tax on good 1 so that $q_1(\alpha) = p_1(\alpha)$ initially. Then choosing $\mu = 1/c$ shows that domestic prices $(1/c)p_1(\alpha)$ and $p_2(\alpha)$ are also consistent with equilibrium. If $q_2(\alpha) = p_2(\alpha) + c$ as with a specific tariff c, this can no longer be done.

C. Equivalance of tariffs and quotas

Any quota which restricts imports of a given commodity independently of the state of nature can be thought of as a collection of state dependent quotas where each quota applies to imports in precisely one state and no others. Similarly, a tariff can be thought of as a collection of state-specific tariffs, each one applied to imports of the given good in one state and no others. Viewed in this general manner it is immediate that any quota, whether state dependent or not, can be exactly duplicated by a state dependent set of tariffs and vice versa. all that is required is that implicit rents from the quota and revenues of the tariff be distributed in the same way.

The problem arises, however, that for many applications one is interested in the use of a tariff or quota which must be chosen *ex ante* before the state of nature is revealed. That is, the level chosen must be state independent. From the discussion above such tariffs and quotas are not really "pure" instruments but rather collections of state-specific tariffs and quotas. In general their effects will be different: an *ad valorem* tariff will differ from a *specific* tariff and both will differ from a quota. In the absence of an equivalency result one can ask which instrument is superior for achieving a given objective. For example, if the objective is limitation of imports to a target level for a small country and state dependent tariffs cannot be used, only a quota can achieve the desired target precisely in all cases. It would therefore be preferable to a tariff which might need to overly restrict trade in some state to achieve the target in others. Even here the conclusion must be modified if the country is not small. The tariff might end up being superior to the quota simply because it tended to restrict trade in a more nearly optimal way than did the quota. One must consider the available policies, the feasible choice set for each policy being considered, and the objective, non-economic or otherwise.

A number of studies have examined the relative efficacy of *ex ante* (state-independent) *ad valorem* tariffs, *ex ante* specific tariffs,

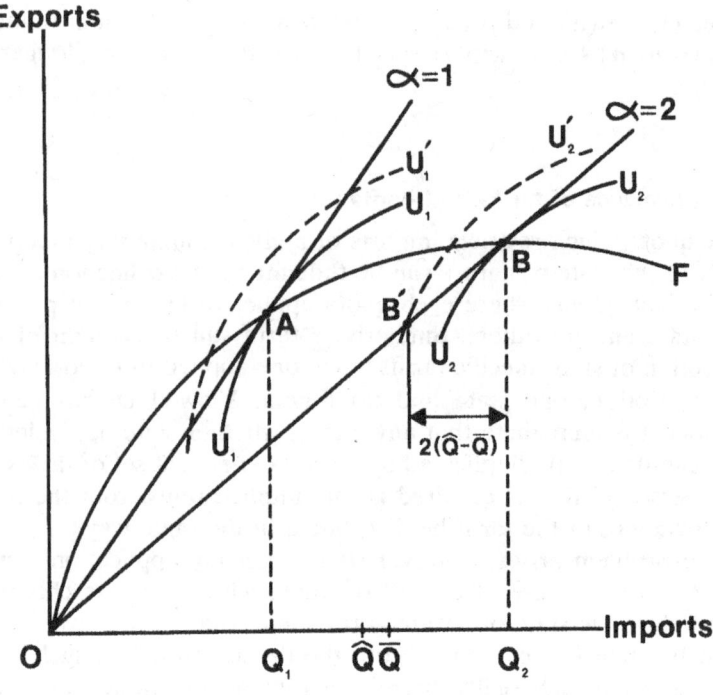

NOTES: High Risk Aversion $\Rightarrow (U_2 - U_2') < (U_1 - U_1')$

FIGURE 6.2 Quota superior to a tariff.

and quotas in achieving reduction of imports to an expected level, an expected value, or for raising an expected amount of revenue.[26] The principles involved are demonstrated in the following two examples which will be explained next. Afterwards we will discuss several unresolved issues.

In the first example we show a situation in which a quota is superior to a tariff in restricting average imports to a target level. In the second example the ranking is reversed and the tariff is superior to a quota. The discussion refers to Figure 6.2 in which the offer curve of the home country is drawn as *OF*. Imports are on the

---

[26] See the bibliographic notes at the end of this chapter.

horizontal axis and exports are on the vertical axis. In the absence of trade restrictions equilibrium trade in each of two states of nature $\alpha = 1, 2$ is given by points A and B, respectively. Q_1 represents domestic imports in state 1 and Q_2 imports in state 2. Both states are equally likely so that average imports are given by $\bar{Q}$ half way between Q_1 and Q_2. The target level of import is $\hat{Q}$ to the left of $\bar{Q}$. The country is small on world markets with the foreign offer curves given by the rays from the origin $O\alpha$ for $\alpha = 1$, $\alpha = 2$ respectively.

Since the country is small on world markets, free trade is optimal. Any reduction in trade from the levels in A or B will therefore reduce welfare from the levels indicated by the respective trade indifference curves U_1 and U_2. A quota will have the effect of reducing trade in state 2 to point B' with welfare U_2'. Expected utility therefore will drop from $(U_1 + U_2)/2$ to $(U_1 + U_2')/2$, a change of $(U_2 - U_2')/2$. A tariff on the other hand will have the effect of reducing trade in both states and welfare will fall as a weighted average of the change in utility in each state. If the loss in welfare in state 1 is very great for a small quantity change, then the quota is preferred to a tariff. For given prices, the degree of change in utility for given budget lines is a function of the degree of risk aversion in the economy. Figure 6.3a draws several budget lines corresponding to prices in state 2 and Figure 6.3b draws the corresponding welfare levels in the case where there is a high degree of risk aversion. Thus the quota achieves the import target with very little loss in welfare ($(U_2 - U_2')/2$ is small) whereas the tariff incurs the much larger loss of which the larger $(U_1 - U_1')/2$ is a part. A quota is superior to a tariff for the objective $\hat{Q}$.

Clearly the degree of risk-aversion, the smallness of the country and the shape of the offer curves all play a role in determining the superior policy tool. The following example relaxes the assumption that the home country is small. In this case the tariff more nearly approximates a state-dependent optimal trade restriction, and decrease in trade is welfare improving. The tariff is now superior to the quota for the objective $\hat{Q}$. The notation is the same as in the previous example except that now U_1' and U_2' represent higher levels of welfare, and the foreign offer curves in states 1 and 2 have curvature. In this case a tariff is superior to a quota in achieving the target average imports $\hat{Q}$ since it causes an increase in trade in state 1 (in the direction to the southeast of point A) at the expense of a

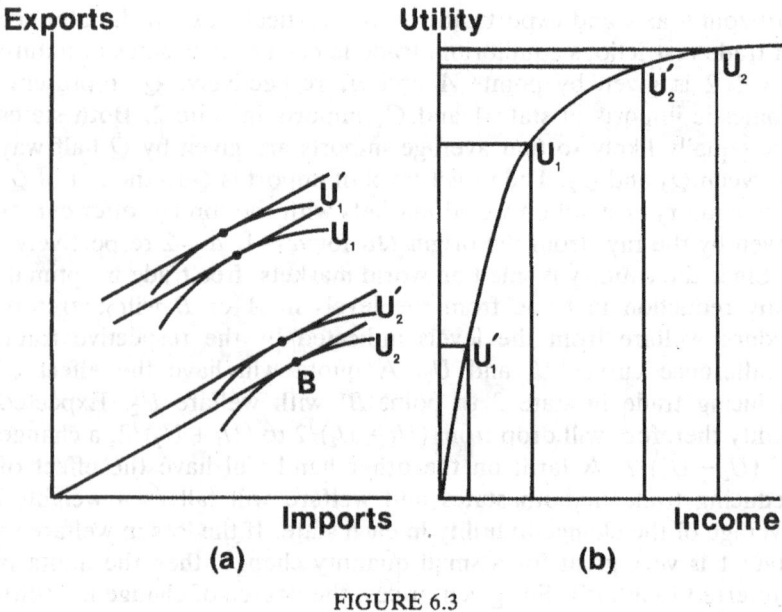

FIGURE 6.3

greater reduction in trade in state 2. Since the welfare gain in state 1 is large and the welfare change in state 2 is small there is a net welfare improvement at the same time that average imports drop. A quota, on the other hand, would reduce imports only in state 2 generating a welfare loss or a smaller welfare gain.

Examples can also be constructed similar to the first one where a tariff is superior to a quota for a small country with sufficiently low risk aversion.

The analysis of policy ranking in the presence of uncertainty is still not well understood, in spite of a number of studies which have made good progress in that direction. This is largely due to the complexity of the problem. Most studies have therefore tended to simplify in some essential respect. In the long run, of course, these simplifying assumptions should be dropped. We mention just two in closing: the choice of objective function and the representation of income generation.

Many of the studies treating the ranking of tariffs and quotas have assumed that the objective is the maximization of expected consumers' surplus. This assumption is inappropriate in most situations

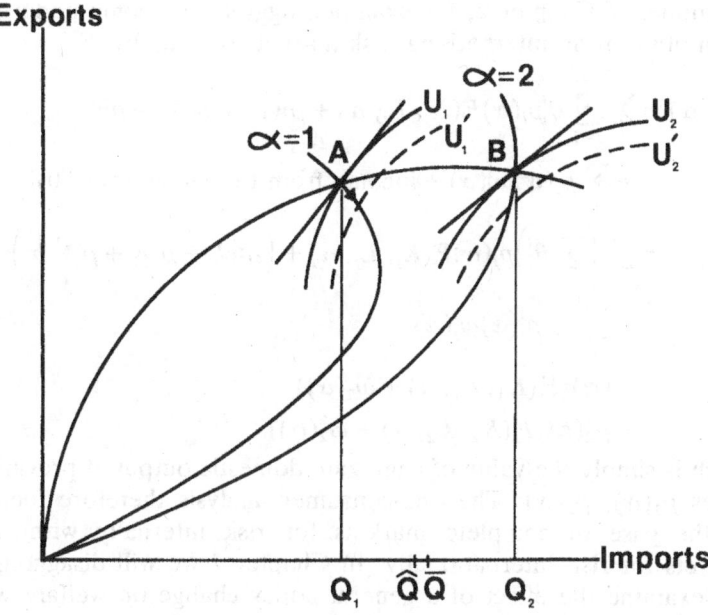

FIGURE 6.4 Tariff superior to a quota.

for two reasons. First, it places restrictions on risk aversion, and second, it ignores the completeness or incompleteness of markets for spreading risk. These affect the utility value of wealth since they imply constraints on how it may be used to purchase final commodities.

Some studies employ the more reasonable expected utility objective function (as the two examples above do) but typically ignore the nature of the internal markets for risk-spreading. Issues of income distribution and internal risk-spreading opportunities as in the Newbery–Stiglitz example of negative gains from trade are therefore totally lacking. The assumption of a country-wide expected utility function implicitly assumes perfect risk-spreading internally and optimal lump sum re-distribution of income. With respect to international markets in risk the common assumption that domestic income is given by a revenue function of the form $r((p_j(\alpha))$ or $r((p_j(\alpha)), \alpha)$ implies the opposite extreme of zero international risk-spreading through foreign ownership of assets. In the model of Chapter 2, for example, aggregate income under the assumption of no international risk markets is given by

$$\sum_i I^i(\alpha) = \sum_i \sum_{j=1}^{2} \theta_j^i p_j(\alpha) F_j(K_j, L_j, \alpha) + \rho w L^i + \rho r K^i + \rho b^i$$

$$+ \sum_j p_j(\alpha) \omega_j^i(\alpha) + \text{income from foreign assets } (=0)$$

$$= \sum_{j=1}^{2} \left(\sum_i \theta_j^i \right) p_j(\alpha) F_j(K_j, L_j, \alpha) + \left(\rho w L + \rho r K + \rho \sum_i b^i \right)$$

$$+ \sum_i \sum_j p_j(\alpha) \omega_j^i(\alpha)$$

$$= p_1(\alpha)(F_1(K_1, L_1, \alpha) + \omega_1(\alpha))$$
$$+ p_2(\alpha)(F_2(K_2, L_2, \alpha) + \omega_2(\alpha))$$

which is simply the value of aggregate domestic output at prevailing prices $p_1(\alpha)$, $p_2(\alpha)$. The one-consumer analysis therefore focuses on the case of complete markets for risk internally with zero markets for risk internationally. In Chapter 7 we will disaggregate and examine the effect of a general policy change on welfare with multiple consumers, international and intranational markets for risk, and incomplete markets.

D. Summary

Under uncertainty a tariff effectively becomes a collection of state-specific tariffs, each one applied to imports of the given commodity in a different state of nature. An *ad valorem* tariff therefore becomes a different policy tool than a quota and both are different from a specific tariff. The results of tariff theory generalize to conditions of uncertainty or not depending on how one interprets the generalization. A specific tariff no longer will substitute for a quota but the appropriate bundle of state-specific tariffs will. Lerner symmetry holds under uncertainty for tariffs treated as state-specific or for *ex ante ad valorem* tariffs but not for *ex ante* fixed specific tariffs.

In comparing *ex ante* policies of quota or tariff, say to achieve a target level of imports, a quota is sometimes preferred to a tariff and sometimes the reverse. The determining factors include the degree of risk aversion of consumers in the home country, the shape of the foreign offer curves and so on. General results allowing for multiple consumers, international ownership of assets, and risk aversion are few.

E. Bibliographic notes

The ranking of tariffs and quotas has been considered by Anderson [1976], Pelcovitz [1976], Dasgupta and Stiglitz [1977], Ohta [1978], Young [1979, 1980], Young and Anderson [1982], Helpman and Razin [1980], and Young and Kemp [1982]. The protective effects of a tariff under uncertainty are treated in Helpman and Razin [1980] and Grinols [1984b].

7. COMMERICAL POLICY

The theory of commerical policy is enlarged by the presence of uncertainty in at least three new dimensions. The effects of policy on the risk-spreading opportunities available to the domestic market, the use of monopoly power in risk markets, and the effect of policy on foreign ownership income (international income distribution effects) are new components which must all be taken into account. Just as an optimal tariff on commodity trade for a large country may improve welfare, so an optimal tariff or tax on foreign capital flows (equity trade) can be used to improve domestic welfare. It is possible that a small country in commodity markets will still gain from a optimal tariff on equity trade. If the opening of trade is not welfare improving because risk-spreading opportunities are reduced, then a tariff employed to restrict trade can act as a partial insurance mechanism to improve welfare. Finally, if countries are linked by international financial flows policy must be re-evaluated. A traditional optimal tariff which achieves gains at the expense of a trading partner whose assets are partly owned by domestic investors may no longer be appropriate since it implies using monopoly power against the assets of home country citizens. Gains in current terms-of-trade advantages must then be weighed against gains (or losses) in foreign assets.

This chapter discusses these issues in terms of the laws of welfare which apply to either the pre-policy equilibrium or post-policy equilibrium depending upon where the comparative statics calculations are made. The relevant expression for welfare change is derived in part A. Part B discusses its use in generating the optimal tariff. The emphasis, however, is on part C which looks more closely at the issue of the policy's effect on the structure of risk-spreading opportunities for the economy.

A. Uncertainty and open-economy welfare

The model of Chapter 3 in many respects resembles a deterministic trade model with distortions. Unless markets for risk are complete the relevant shadow prices vary across different agents and, if restrictions on international trade in commodities and securities are introduced, across different countries. The effects of a change in commerical policy must then be gauged in terms of the agent involved.

Proceeding in a stepwise fashion, set up the Lagrangian for the ith individual,

$$\mathcal{L}^i = U^i(I^i; p) + \lambda^i \left[\sum_j \bar{\theta}^i_j(P_j - wL_j - rK_j) - \sum_j \theta^i_j P_j - b^i \right]. \quad (7.1)$$

Totally differentiate $\mathcal{L}^i$, invoking the envelope theorem with respect to θ^i_j, b^i to obtain,

$$dU^i = \sum_\alpha U^i_\alpha (\sum_j \theta^i_j d(p_j F_j) + d\rho w L^i + d\rho r K^i + d\rho b^i$$

$$+ \sum_j dp_j(\alpha) \omega^i_j(\alpha) + dT^i)$$

$$+ \sum_\alpha \sum_j (\partial U^i / \partial p_j(\alpha)) \, dp_j(\alpha)$$

$$+ \lambda^i \left[\sum_j \theta^i_j (dP_j - dwL_j - drK_j) - \sum_j \theta^i_j dP_j \right].$$

Simplifying and re-arranging using first order conditions from the consumer's portfolio choice problem,

$$(1/\sum_\alpha U^i_\alpha \rho) \, dU^i = \sum_\alpha \beta^i(\alpha) \left[\sum_j \theta^i_j \, d\rho_j(\alpha) F_j(K_j, L_j, \alpha) + dT^i(\alpha) \right]$$
$$+ ((\omega^i_1(\alpha) - x^i_1(\alpha))) \, dp_1(\alpha)$$
$$+ (\omega^i_2(\alpha) - x^i_2(\alpha)) \, dp_2(\alpha))/\rho + \sum_j \bar{\theta}^i_j \, dP_j$$
$$+ d\left(\rho w \left(L^i - \sum_j \bar{\theta}^i_j L_j\right) + \rho r \left(K^i - \sum_j \theta^i_j K_j\right)\right)/\rho$$
$$- \sum_j \theta^i_j \left(\sum_\alpha d(\beta(\alpha) p_j(\alpha)) F_j(K_j, L_j, \alpha)\right)$$
$$+ \sum_j \theta^i_j \sum_\alpha \gamma^i(\alpha) p_j(\alpha) \, dF_j(K_j, L_j, \alpha).^{27} \qquad (7.2)$$

where $dT^i(\alpha)$ is the change in transfers to individual i out of tariff revenues (if any), $x^i_1(\alpha)$, $x^i_2(\alpha)$ are consumption of goods 1 and 2 in future state α and $\gamma^i(\alpha)$ and $\beta(\alpha)$ are defined by

$$\beta^i(\alpha) = \beta(\alpha) + \gamma^i(\alpha)$$

where $\beta(\alpha)$ is chosen so that $\sum_\alpha \beta(\alpha) p_j(\alpha) F_j(K_j, L_j, \alpha) = P_j$ for all j. The reason for breaking $\beta^i(\alpha)$ into two components $\beta(\alpha)$ and $\gamma^i(\alpha)$ will be discussed in part C.[28] We will refer to Eq. (7.2) in the remainder of this chapter.

The complexity of the expression for dU^i is an unavoidable consequence of the greater complexity of the trade model under uncertainty with incomplete markets. Nevertheless, the terms of (7.2) can be sorted out and a great deal of order be brought to bear in understanding how a policy change affects welfare. An increase in spot prices $p_1(\alpha)$, $p_2(\alpha)$ affects welfare through two routes. $(\omega^i_1 - x^i_1) \, dp_1(\alpha) + (\omega^i_2 - x^i_2) \, dp_2(\alpha)$ shows the welfare change due to the change in cost of net purchases of both goods for consumption. $\sum_\alpha \beta^i(\alpha) \theta^i_j \, dp_j(\alpha) F_j(K_j, L_j, \alpha)$ represents the increased income in state α from ownership of the securities of firm j, while

---

[27] (7.2) expresses dU^i in units of present value wealth—hence the need to divide by $\sum_i U^i_\alpha \rho$.

[28] Notice that $\sum_\alpha \gamma^i(\alpha)[p_j(\alpha) F_j] = \sum_\alpha \beta^i(\alpha) p_j(\alpha) F_j - \sum_\alpha \beta(\alpha) p_j(\alpha) F_j = P_j - P_j = 0$ follows from the construction of $\beta(\alpha)$.

$\sum_j (\bar{\theta}^i_j dP_j - \theta^i_j \sum_\alpha d(\beta(\alpha)p_j(\alpha))F_j(K_j, L_j, \alpha))$ is the net effect of the price change on the consumer's ability to purchase security j. The stock market price of security j, dP_j, of course, changes due to the changes in future prices $p_j(\alpha)$ at which firm j may sell its output. Insofar as $\sum_j \bar{\theta}^i_j dP_j$ is positive (the consumer owns a more valuable asset) the consumer as investor is better off. Insofar as $\sum_\alpha d(\beta(\alpha)p_j(\alpha))F_j$ is positive the consumer/investor is worse off since he must purchase more costly assets. $\sum_\alpha \beta^i(\alpha) dT^i(\alpha)$ is the value of income distribution from tariff revenues to consumer i.

The only remaining terms in (7.2) are $d(\rho w(L^i - \sum_j \bar{\theta}^i_j L_j) + \rho r(K^i - \sum_j \bar{\theta}^i_j K_j))/\rho$ and $\sum_j \theta^i_j \sum_\alpha \gamma^i(\alpha) dF_j(K_j, L_j, \alpha)$. The first of these relates to the consumer as an owner of factor services. The individual owns L^i, K^i services of labor and capital (supplying them) but through firm ownership is obligated to payments for $\bar{\theta}^i_j K_j$, $\bar{\theta}^i_j L_j$ (purchasing them) so that the net effect on welfare of a change in w, r depends on whether the individual is a net buyer or seller. The last term relates to the effect of the policy on influencing risk-spreading opportunities and will be discussed in section C.

B. Optimal tariffs and commercial policy

The optimal tariff can be derived from (7.2) by evaluating dU^i at the final equilibrium position and setting dU^i equal to zero. Depending on the feasible tools, a number of types of optimal tariffs can be derived.

For example, if the tariff is restricted to be state independent and specific the difference between the future domestic spot prices $p_j(\alpha)$ and foreign prices will be a constant. Total tariff revenues will be given by that constant times imports in the given state of nature. On the other hand, if the tariff can be state dependent then the level of the tariff for each state becomes a choice variable and $dU^i/dt(\alpha) = 0$ becomes a system of equations which must be solved for $(t(\alpha))$. If taxes or trade in securities are imposed, then $dT^i(\alpha)$ should also include distribution of tax revenues from security taxes and so on.

As an example, let us simplify using (7.2) to the familiar case of the optimal tariff under certainty. If there is only one future state of nature (there is certainty) $\beta^i(\alpha) = 1/\rho$ for all i and $\gamma^i(\alpha) \equiv 0$. Sum

(7.2) over the households in the domestic country to get

$$\sum_i \left(1 \bigg/ \sum_i U^i_\alpha\right) dU^i = [dP_1 + dP_2] + dT - (x_1\, dp_1 - x_2\, dp_2)$$
$$= y_1\, dp_1 + y_2\, dp_2 + d(t(x_i - y_1)) - x_1\, dp_1 - x_2\, dp_2$$
$$= -E_1\, dp_1 + d(tE_1) \qquad (7.3)$$

where the last equality follows from choice of good 2 as numeraire with initial prices equal to unity (assume $\omega^i_j(\alpha) = 0$ as in the deterministic model). Setting (7.3) equal to zero and solving for t, using the fact that E_1 must lie on the foreign offer curve generates the formula for the optimal tariff as in the usual analysis,

$$-E_1 dp_1 - d(p_1 - p_1^*)E_1^* = 0$$
$$-t\frac{dE_1^*}{dp_1^*} + E_1^* = 0$$
$$t = 1/\eta^*$$

where $\eta^* = \dfrac{dE_1^*}{dp_1^*}\dfrac{P_1^*}{E_1^*}$ is the elasticity of foreign supply and superscript * denotes the foreign variable. More intricate policy options can be analyzed in the same way.[29]

C. Risk spreading effects of policy

We now turn to the main concern of this chapter which is an evaluation of the risk spreading effects of policy. Throughout our

---

[29] The following example shows the joint setting of two policy tools, optimal tariff plus tax on capital imports. Assuming F represents domestic imports of capital services it can be shown that domestic welfare is proportional to $(y_2 - x_2) dp_2^* + (p_2 - p_2^*) dx_d + (p_2^* - p_{2t}) dy_2 - F\, dr^* + (r - r^*) dF$ where r^* is the foreign rental rate on capital and p_{2t} is the domestic rate of transformation between goods 1 and 2. Choosing the optimal tariff jointly with optimal tax on capital import implies the two first order conditions

$$0 = (y_2 - x_2)\frac{dp_2^*}{dy_2} + (p_2 - p_2^*) + (p_2^* - p_{2t})\frac{dy_2}{dx_2} - F\frac{dr^*}{dx_2}$$

$$0 = (y_2 - x_2)\frac{dp_2^*}{dy_2} + (p_2^* - p_{2t})\frac{dy_2}{dF} - F\frac{dr^*}{dF} + (r - r^*)$$

where x_2 and F are the home country choice variables. Solving for $r - r^*$ and $p_2 - p_2^*$ gives the formula for optimal tax on capital services and tariff, etc. See Kemp [1966] or Gehrels [1971].

study of uncertainty and the theory of international trade we have emphasized the importance of the structure of the security market for determining welfare. If markets are incomplete the span of the set of traded securities determines the set within which investors can trade risk between themselves. If this set changes, because firm production choices have changed, the traded securities will span a different region of return space. To some investors this shift will be beneficial, to others perhaps not. Describing the corresponding measure of welfare change is the purpose of this section.

Several observations are useful at the outset. We begin with the case of least risk spreading opportunity and progress to the greatest. If there is no trade in risky securities each investor or group of investors is constrained to accept the profile of risk generated by the firm he (or they) own directly. The representative model here might be that of a series of farmers (individual entrepreneurs) who commit resources before the state of nature is known and receive a random payoff after the state is revealed. Return versus risk is internally weighed and converted into a production choice which generates welfare.

In contrast, if there are markets in risk but they are incomplete, a change in the environment can be broken down separately into its effect on the income generated by the assets owned by the investor, the prices he must pay for assets and commodities, and the separate effect on his ability to insure himself (risk-spread) in the available risk markets. Equation (7.2) can be used to discuss this type of separation. If markets are complete, or if the space spanned by traded securities never changes,[30] we would expect to see no separate welfare effect from changes in risk spreading opportunities. In the case of perfect markets risk spreading opportunities are always the unchanging full return space. In the case of fixed spanning, risk spreading opportunities are exogenously constrained never to change. The separate welfare effect due to altered risk spreading opportunities should therefore drop out. This is indeed what happens.

Gathering the terms of (7.2) which relate explicitly to the

---

[30] For example, this occurs if production uncertainty takes the special multiplicative form.

portfolio holdings of investor i we have,

$$\sum_j \bar{\theta}^i_j dP_j - \sum_j \theta^i_j d(\beta(\alpha)p_j(\alpha))F_j(K_j, L_j, \alpha)$$
$$+ \sum_j \theta^i_j \sum_\alpha \gamma^i(\alpha)p_j(\alpha) dF_j(K_j, L_j, \alpha). \quad (7.4)$$

The other terms deal with income or price effects in future states of nature, or factor income.

The first two terms in (7.4) have been discussed briefly in part A. We expand on that here to show first how monopoly power in risk markets is treated and then changes in risk spreading opportunities. From the pricing relation for risky assets and the construction of $\beta(\alpha)$ we have,

$$P_j = \sum_\alpha \beta(\alpha)p_j(\alpha)F_j$$

thus

$$dP_j = \underbrace{\sum_\alpha \beta(\alpha)p_j(\alpha) dF_j}_{(a)} + \underbrace{\sum_\alpha d(\beta(\alpha)p_j(\alpha))F_j}_{(b)}$$

where part (b) represents increased value of asset j due to the effect of the policy on risk prices $\beta(\alpha)$ and spot prices $p_j(\alpha)$. Making use of this monopoly power by the home country, however, must be tempered by the knowledge that purchasers of the asset may be domestic households. Hence the price effects on domestic purchases $\sum_j \theta^i_j d(\beta(\alpha)p_j(\alpha))F_j$ are subtracted from $\sum_j \bar{\theta}^i dP_j$ to leave the net welfare effect of a monopolistic price increase in spot markets and risk markets as hown in (7.4).

For simplicity, now assume that all assets are held domestically so that (7.4) becomes,

$$\sum_j \sum_\alpha \beta(\alpha)p_j(\alpha) dF_j + \sum_j \sum_\alpha \gamma^i(\alpha)p_j(\alpha) dF_j \quad (7.5)$$

Inspection of (7.5) shows that it equals $\sum_j \sum_\alpha \beta^i(\alpha)p_j(\alpha) dF_j$, part of which has been attributed to welfare gains from real increased asset value. The change in dF_j has another component in addition to size, however, and that is its potentially new stochastic profile as a vehicle for risk spreading. If $\beta^i(\alpha)$ is split so as to keep all welfare gains due to improved risk-spreading in $\gamma^i(\alpha)$, then

$\Sigma_j \Sigma_\alpha \gamma^i(\alpha) p_j(\alpha) \, dF_j$ represents the marginal welfare effect of a new set of traded securities available for trade in risk markets. If dF_j is a linear combination of already traded assets (as is the case if markets are complete or production uncertainty is multiplicative) then $\Sigma_j \Sigma_\alpha \gamma^i(\alpha) P_j(\alpha) \, dF_j \equiv 0$.

The split of $\beta^i(\alpha)$ into two components is a device to represent the separate welfare effect of improved risk spreading opportunities. We now give an example of how it works.

EXAMPLE Assume that investor utility, $U^i(I^i, p)$ takes the special form

$$U^i = U^i(E^i, V^i, p) \tag{7.6}$$

where

$$E^i = \sum_\alpha \pi_\alpha I^i(\alpha)$$

$$V^i = \sum_\alpha \pi_\alpha (I^i(\alpha) - E^i)^2$$

and π_α is the probability that state α will occur. (7.6) is familiar from the mean-variance model of portfolio choice. We do not discuss its merits here but only use it as a convenient example. It is particularly useful for that purpose because it has a well-defined and easily interpretable measure of risk.[31] For the example, write

$$I^i(\alpha) = \sum_j \theta^i_j P_j(\alpha) F_j + f^i T + \rho w L^i + \rho r K^i + \rho b^i$$

where f^i is individual i's fractional endowment share of T, $T = p_1(\alpha)\omega_1(\alpha) + p_2(\alpha)\omega_2(\alpha)$. The first order conditions to the consumer's portfolio problem are the same as in Chapter 2 except that it is now possible to write out $\beta^i(\alpha)$ explicitly in terms of the relevant moments of the investor's portfolio.

Use matrix notation to write,

$$E^i = (\theta^i)'\bar{R} + \rho b^i + \rho w L^i + \rho r K^i + f^i \bar{T}$$

$$V^i = (\theta^i)' \sum \theta^i + (\theta^i)' H f^i$$

---

[31] The conclusions of this model can also be derived in the continuous time framework, e.g., Grinols [1984c].

where θ^i is the column vector whose elements are θ^i_j, R is a column vector with components $R_j = p_j(\alpha)F_j$ and $\bar{R}$ is the column vector whose elements are the expected return $\sum_\alpha \pi_\alpha P_j(\alpha)F_j$, and $\bar{T}$ is the expected value of T. Σ is the variance-convariance matrix of the returns $p_j(\alpha)F_j$, and H is the column vector of covariances between T and $p_j(\alpha)F_j$. First order conditions for Max U^i such that $\sum_j \bar{\theta}^i_j(P_j - wL_j - rK_j) = \sum_j \theta^i_j P_j + b^i$ are

$$U^i_E \binom{\bar{R}}{\rho} + 2U^i_v \binom{\Sigma \theta^i + f^i H}{0} = \lambda^i \binom{P}{1}, \qquad (7.7')$$

which implies

$$P = \frac{1}{\rho}\left(\bar{R} + \frac{1}{\delta}\left(\sum \Phi + H\right)\right) \qquad (7.7a)$$

$$\theta^i = \varepsilon^i \Phi + (\varepsilon^i - f^i)\Sigma^{-1} H \qquad (7.7b)$$

where $\delta = \sum_i \delta^i$, $\delta^i = U^i_E/2U^i_V$, $\varepsilon^i = \delta^i/\delta$, and Φ is a conformable column vector of ones. Substituting for θ^i into $\partial U^i/\partial I^i(\alpha) = U^i_E \pi_\alpha + 2U^i_V(I^i(\alpha) - E^i)$ and solving for $\beta^i(\alpha)$ gives,

$$\beta^i(\alpha) = \frac{1}{\rho}\pi_\alpha\left[1 + \frac{1}{\delta}(\Phi'(R - \bar{R}) + (T - \bar{T}))\right]$$

$$+ \frac{1}{\rho}\pi_\alpha \frac{(f^i - \varepsilon^i)}{\delta^i}((T - \bar{T}) - H'\Sigma^{-1}(R - \bar{R})).^{32} \qquad (7.8)$$

$\beta^i(\alpha)$ naturally breaks down into the sum of two components,

$$\beta^i(\alpha) = \beta(\alpha) + \gamma^i(\alpha)$$

where

$$\beta(\alpha) = \frac{1}{\rho}\left[\pi_\alpha\left(1 + \frac{1}{\delta}(\Phi'(R - \bar{R}) + (T - \bar{T}))\right)\right]$$

$$\gamma^i(\alpha) = \frac{1}{\rho}\left[\pi_\alpha(f^i - \varepsilon^i)\frac{1}{\delta^i}\left((T - \bar{T}) - H'\Sigma^{-1}(R - \bar{R})\right)\right]. \qquad (7.9)$$

---

[32] Derivations of (7.7) and (7.8) are given in the appendix to this chapter.

By direct computation and comparison to (7.7)

$$\sum_\alpha \beta(\alpha)R_j = \sum_\alpha \beta(\alpha)p_j(\alpha)F_j(K_j, L_j, \alpha)$$

$$= \frac{1}{\rho}\left[\bar{R}_j + \frac{1}{\delta}\text{Cov}\left(\sum_j R_j + T, R_j\right)\right]$$

$$= P_j \qquad (7.10)$$

where $\text{Cov}(\cdot,\cdot)$ denotes covariance. The second equality in equation (7.10) is recognized as the standard mean-variance pricing formula for capital assets. Similarly

$$\sum_\alpha \gamma^i(\alpha)R_j = (f^i - \varepsilon^i)\frac{1}{(\delta^i\rho)}[\text{Cov}(T, R_j) - H'\Sigma^{-1}\Sigma_j]$$

$$= (f^i - \varepsilon^i)\frac{1}{(\delta^i\rho)}[H_j - H'\Sigma^{-1}\Sigma_j]$$

where H_j is the jth element of H and Σ_j is the jth column of Σ. Thus

$$\sum_\alpha \gamma^i(\alpha)R_j = (f^i - \varepsilon^i)/(\delta^i\rho)[H_j - H_j] = 0. \qquad (7.11)$$

$\beta(\alpha)$ and $\gamma^i(\alpha)$ as defined in (7.9) therefore correspond to $\beta(\alpha)$ and $\gamma^i(\alpha)$ in the general model. In that model we said that

$$\sum_\alpha \gamma^i(\alpha)p_j(\alpha)\,dF_j$$

represented the welfare effect of the policy from changing the set of commodities available for spreading risk. Looking at the components of $\gamma^i(\alpha)$ using (7.9), the constant $(f^i - \varepsilon^i)/\rho\delta^i$ converts future period units of variance into present-value wealth terms. $u_\alpha \equiv (T - \bar{T}) - H'\Sigma^{-1}(R - \bar{R})$ is recognized as the residual from a regression of deviations of T from its mean on the returns of traded securities (in deviation from their mean). The regression coefficients are given by $\Sigma^{-1}H$.[33] $\sum_\alpha \pi_\alpha[(T - \bar{T}) - H'\Sigma^{-1}(R - \bar{R})][P_j\,dF_j]$ is therefore the covariance between $p_j\,dF_j$ and the residual u_α. Since the residual from a regression is always orthogonal to the explanatory variables this explains why $\text{cov}(u, R_j) = 0$ as shown in (7.10) above.

Accordingly, the description of how changes in the contract

---

[33] This corresponds to the familiar $(X'X)^{-1}X'Y$ formula for coefficients from an ordinary least squares regression of Y on the variable X.

structure affect welfare is as follows: The investor seeks to spread his portfolio risk by diversifying. In the mean variance context this means that he wishes to hold ultimately the fraction ε^i of the market portfolio and the riskless asset. Because markets are not complete he must use the best available market "replica" of $f^i T$ to diversify his holdings of endowment income to the desired level ε^i. He therefore buys $(\varepsilon^i - f^i)$ units of the market replica of T (given by the regression described above) to add to his endowment. With his purchase of the market portfolio and riskless asset, this leaves him as close to his desired portfolio (and holding of risk) as the market allows. Should the market structure change to allow the replica of T to improve he will have available better risk spreading opportunities and his welfare will rise *ceteris paribus*. The requirement that a new asset allow better replication of T is precisely the condition that $p_j(\alpha)\, dF_j$ be correlated with the residual u.[34]

To close, we now show in the example why a model with complete markets, or multiplicative production uncertainty, can never have any welfare effects operating through improved risk spreading opportunities. The first case is simple. u_α is identically zero since, with complete markets, hedging or replication of T is perfect. In insurance terms this says that the available insurance for any risk is perfect since the market regression is an exact fit. Thus, perfect insurance in asset markets cannot be improved upon and the required covariance is always identically zero as required by $u_\alpha \equiv 0$. In the case of multiplicative production uncertainty, production across states of nature is always a scalar multiple of a fixed vector. dF_j is therefore a multiple of F_j and $\text{cov}(u, dF_j) = \text{cov}(u, F_j) = 0$. The model indicates that whatever choices are made for production there is no effect on risk spreading opportunities. This agrees with the fact that the space spanned by traded securities, which determines the ability to spread risk, is invariant.

D. Summary

Commercial policy for an open country facing uncertainty involves several features not found in a deterministic setting. Among these

---

[34] See any econometrics textbook. The argument is equivalent to the requirement that the new asset improve R^2 of the regression of T on traded assets.

are the possibility of monopoly power in risk markets and the ability of policy to influence risk-spreading opportunities of the market. These were examined briefly and a measure of the marginal welfare effects presented.

E. Bibliographic notes

The types of commerical policy questions which are open to a country under uncertainty are too great to do justice in a few references. However, Newbery and Stiglitz [1981] discuss in depth a number of issues relating to open-economy commerical policy. Grossman and Razin [1984] discuss some interesting features of factor mobility under uncertainty. This work relates to the earlier literature on commerical policy for countries trading in factor services, cf. Kemp [1966], Gehrels [1971]. The material from this section was taken partly from Grinols [1985b]. Eaton and Grossman [1981], in a paper discussed by Pomery [1984], discuss the use of tariffs to compensate for imperfect internal risk-sharing under a number of interesting alternatives.

Appendix

Derivation of Eq (7.7) and (7.8)

Divide (7.7') by $2U_j^i$ and sum over i to get,

$$\sum_i \delta^i \binom{\bar{R}}{\rho} + \binom{\sum \Phi + H}{0} = \sum \lambda^i/2U_V^i \binom{P}{1} \qquad (A7.1)$$

Solve for P using the fact that $\rho\delta^i = \lambda^i/2U_j^i$ to get (7.7a). Substitute (A7.1) into (7.7'), again using the relation that $\rho\delta^i = \lambda^i/2U_V^i$ to get

$$\delta^i \bar{R} + \sum \theta^i + f^i H = \rho\delta^i \left(\bar{R} + \left(1 / \sum_i \delta^i \right) \sum \Phi + H \right)$$

Multiplying both sides by Σ^{-1} and collecting terms gives (7.7b).

To derive (7.8) differentiate U^i to get

$$U_\alpha^1 = \pi_\alpha U_E^i + \pi_\alpha (2U_V^i)(I^i(\alpha) - E^i).$$

Substituting for $I^i(\alpha) - E^i$ in matrix notation and collecting terms,

$$U^i_\alpha = \pi_\alpha(2U^i_V)[\delta^i + [(\theta^i)(R - \bar{R}) + f^i(T - \bar{T})]]. \quad \text{(A7.2)}$$

Substitute (7.7b) into (A7.2) adding and subtracting terms to get,

$$U^i_\alpha = \pi_\alpha(2U^i_V)\delta^i[1 + 1/\delta(\Phi'(R - \bar{R}) + (T - \bar{T}))]$$
$$+ \pi_\alpha(2U^i_V)(f^i - \varepsilon^i)[(T - \bar{T}) - H'\Sigma^{-1}(R - \bar{R})]. \quad \text{(A7.3)}$$

Sum (A7.3) over α to get

$$\sum_\alpha U^i_\alpha \rho = (2U^i_V)\delta^i\rho \quad \text{(A7.4)}$$

Using (A7.4) to divide U^i_α by $\sum_\alpha U^i_\alpha \rho$ gives (7.8).

References

Anderson, J. E. (1976), "Optimal Buffering Policies for a Small Trading Country," *Southern Economic Journal*, 43, 1067–1076.

Arrow, Kenneth J. (1964), "The Role of Securities in the Optimal Allocation of Risk-bearing," *Review of Economic Studies*, 31, 91–96.

Arrow, Kenneth J. (1970), *Essays in the Theory of Risk-bearing* (Chicago: Markham).

Arrow, Kenneth J. and Frank H. Hahn (1971), *General Competitive Analysis* (San Francisco: Holden-Day, Inc.).

Baron, David P. and Robert Forsythe (1979), "Models of the Firm and International Trade Under Uncertainty," *American Economic Review*, 69, 565–574.

Batra, Raveendra (1974), "Resource Allocation in a General Equilibrium Model of Production Under Uncertainty," *Journal of Economic Theory*, 8, 50–63.

Batra, Raveendra (1975), *The Pure Theory of International Trade Under Uncertainty* (New York: Halstead Press).

Chang, Winston W., Wilfred J. Ethier and Murray C. Kemp (1980). "The Theorems of International Trade with Joint Production," *Journal of International Economics*, 10, 377–394.

Dasgupta, Partha and Joseph E. Stiglitz (1977), "Tariffs versus Quotas as Revenue Raising Devices," *American Economic Review*, 67, 975–981.

Debreu, Gerard (1959), *Theory of Value*, (New Haven: Yale University Press).

DeAngelo, H. (1981), "Competition and Unanimity," *American Economic Review*, 71, 18–27.

Diamond, Peter A. (1967), "The Role of a Stock Market in a General Equilibrium Model with Technological Uncertainty," *American Economic Review*, 57, 759–776.

Drèze, Jacques H. (1974), "Investment under Private Ownership: Optimality, Equilibrium and Stability," in J. H. Drèze (ed.), *Allocation Under Uncertainty: Equilibrium and Optimality* (New York: John Wiley).

Dumas, Bernard (1980), "The Theorems of International Trade under Generalized Uncertainty," *Journal of International Economics*, 10, 481–498.

Eaton, Jonathan and Gene M. Grossman (1981), "Tariffs as Insurance: Optimal Commerical Policy When Domestic Markets are Incomplete," Working Paper 797, National Bureau of Economic Research.

Ekern, Steinar and Robert Wilson (1974), "On the Theory of the Firm in an Economy with Incomplete Markets," *The Bell Journal of Economics and Management Science*, **5**, 1, 171-180.

Fries, Timothy (1983), "The Possibility of an Immiserizing Transfer Under Uncertainty," *Journal of International Economics*, **15**, 3/4, 297-312.

Fries, Timothy (1984), "Uncertainty as a Possible Rationale for Customs Unions," *Journal of International Economics*, **17**, 3/4, 347-358.

Gehrels, F. (1971), "Optimal Restrictions on Foreign Trade and Investment," *American Economic Review*, **61**, 147-159.

Grandmont, Jean-Michel and Daniel McFadden (1972), "A Technical Note on Classical Gains from Trade," *Journal of International Economics*, **2**, 2, 109-125.

Grinols, Earl L. (1984a), "Competition and Optimal Departures from Stock Market Value Maximization by Firms," *Journal of Economic Dynamics and Control*, **8**, 3, December, 277-289.

Grinols, Earl L. (1984b), "Spot Market-Risk Market Interaction and the Protective Effects of a Tariff Under Uncertainty," *The Economic Journal*, **94**, 373, March, 95-103.

Grinols, Earl L. (1984c), "Production and Risk Leveling in the Intertemporal Capital Asset Pricing Model," *The Journal of Finance*, **39**, 5, December, 1571-1595.

Grinols, Earl L. (1985a), "International Trade and Incomplete Markets," *Economica*, **52**, 206, May, 245-255.

Grinols, Earl L. (1985b), "Trade, Distortions and Welfare Under Uncertainty," *Oxford Economic Papers*, **37**, 3, September, 362-374.

Grossman, Sanford and Oliver Hart (1979), "A Theory of Competitive Equilibrium in Stock Market Economics," *Econometrica*, **47**, 2, 293-330.

Grossman, Sanford and Joseph Stiglitz (1980), "Stockholder Unanimity in Making Production and Financial Decisions," *Quarterly Journal of Economics*, **44**, 3, 543-566.

Grossman, Gene M. and Assaf Razin (1984), "International Capital Movements Under Uncertainty," *Journal of Political Economy*, **92**, 286-306.

Helpman, Elhanan and Assaf Razin (1978), *A Theory of International Trade Under Uncertainty* (New York: Academic Press).

Kemp, Murray C. (1966), "The Gain from International Trade and Investment: A Neo-Heckscher-Ohlin Approach," *American Economic Review*, **56**, 4, 788-809.

Kemp, Murray C. (1976), *Three Topics in the Theory of International Trade: Distribution, Welfare and Uncertainty* (Amsterdam: North-Holland).

Kemp, Murray C. and N. Liviatan (1973), "Production and Trade Patterns Under Uncertainty," *Economic Record*, **49**, 215-227.

Kemp, Murray C. and Henry Wan, Jr. (1972), "The Gain from Free Trade," *International Economic Review*, **13**, 3.

Kemp, Murray C. and Henry Wan, Jr. (1987), "The Gains from Trade," *Fundamentals of Pure and Applied Economics* (forthcoming).

Kemp, Murray C. and Hiroshi Ohta (1978), "The Optimal Level of Exports Under Threat of Foreign Import Restriction," *Canadian Journal of Economics*, **11**, 720-725.

Kemp, Murray C. and Horoshi Ohta (1979), "Some Implications of Uncertainty in a Small Open Economy," *Economic Record*, **55**, 354-358.

Kemp, Murray C. and Michihizo Ohyama (1978), "The Gain from Free Trade

Under Conditions of Uncertainty," *Journal of International Economics*, **8**, 139-141.

Kemp, Murray C., Ngo Van Long and Koji Okuguchi (1981), "On the Possibility of Deriving Conclusions of Stolper-Samuelson Type when Commodity Prices are Random," *The Economic Studies Quarterly*, XXXII, **2**, 111-115.

Leland, Hayne E. (1974), "Production Theory and the Stock Market," *The Bell Journal of Economics and Management Science*, **5**, 1, 125-144.

Lerner, Abba (1936), "The Symmetry between Import and Export Taxes," *Economica*, **3**, 11, 306-313.

Metzler, Lloyd (1946), "Tariffs, the Terms of Trade and the Distribution of National Income," *Journal of Political Economy*, **57**, 1, 1-29.

Newbery, David M. G. and Joseph E. Stiglitz (1981), *The Theory of Commodity Price Stabilization: A Study in the Economics of Risk* (Oxford: Oxford University Press).

Newbery, David M. G. and Joseph E. Stiglitz (1984), "Pareto Inferior Trade," *The Review of Economic Studies*, **51**, 1. 164, 1-12.

Nielsen, Nils C. (1976), "The Investment Decision of the Firm Under Uncertainty and the Allocative Efficiency of Capital Markets," *The Journal of Finance*, **31**, 2, 587-604.

Ohta, Hiroshi (1978), "On the Ranking of Price and Quantity Controls Under Uncertainty," *Journal of International Economics*, **8**, 4, 543-550.

Pelcovits, Michael (1976), "Quotas versus Tariffs," *Journal of International Economics*, **6**, 363-370.

Pomery, John (1976), "International Trade and Uncertainty: Simple General Equilibrium Models Involving Randomness," Ph.D. Dissertation, University of Rochester.

Pomery, John, "Uncertainty and International Trade," in *International Economic Policy*, Rudiger Dornbusch and Jacob A. Frenkel, eds. (Baltimore: The Johns Hopkins Press, 1979).

Pomery, John, "Uncertainty in Trade Models," in *Handbook of International Economics*, Vol. I. R. W. Jones and P. B. Kenen, eds. (Amsterdam: Elsevier Science Publishers, 1984).

Pomery, John (1983), "Restricted Stock Markets in Simple General Equilibrium Models with Production Uncertainty," *Journal of International Economics*, **15**, 253-276.

Radner, Roy (1974), "A Note on Unanimity of Stockholders' Preferences Among Alternative Production Plans," *The Bell Journal of Economics and Management Science*, **5**, 1, 181-186.

Stiglitz, Joseph E. (1982), "The Inefficiency of the Stock Market Equilibrium," *The Review of Economic Studies*, **49**, 2, 156, 241-262.

Young, Leslie (1984), "Uncertainty and the Theory of International Trade in Long Run Equilibrium," *Journal of Economic Theory*, **32**, 1, 67-92.

Young, Leslie (1979), "Ranking Optimal Tariffs and Quotas for a Large Country Under Uncertainty," *Journal of International Economics*, **9**, 249-264.

Young, Leslie (1980), "Tariffs versus Quotas Under Uncertainty: An Extension," *American Economic Review*, **70**, 522-527.

Young, Leslie and James E. Anderson (1982), "Risk Aversion and Optimal Trade Restrictions," *The Review of Economic Studies*, **49**, 291-305.

Young, Leslie and Murray C. Kemp (1982), "On the Optimal Stabilization of International Producers' Prices in International Trade," *International Economic Review*. **23**. 123-141.

INDEX

Allocations, welfare properties of 59
Autarky
  definition with foreign ownership and uncertainty 51
  welfare relative to free trade 54
Capital
  payment for services 7
  intensities and prices 49
Commercial Policy 77
  effect of policy on risk sharing 79, 81
  monopoly power in risk markets 83
  monopoly power in spot markets 84
  optimal tariffs under uncertainty 80
Complete markets 16, 17
  consumer choices 5, 10–11, 17
Cone of diversification and factor price equalization 40
Constrained Pareto Optima 59, 60
Country 5

Elementary security 7
Elements of the economy 4
  allocation 5, 6
  commodities 4
  consumers 5
  firms 4
Equilibria under uncertainty, welfare properties of 59
Ex ante vs. *ex post* shareholder objectives 20, 21

Factor, market clearing 8
Factor price equalization 36
  cone of diversification and factor price equalization 40, 41

factor price equalization and global univalence 38
factor price equalization and international trade in securities 39
failure even with trade in securities 39
Factor price response 48, 49
Firm
  choice rule in incomplete markets 20
  choice rule in perfect markets 17
  choice rule with no risk markets 25
  competitive-like behavior in risk markets 19
  first order conditions 8, 20, 26
  production output 4, 5
  state dependent profits 5
Free trade, welfare relative to autarky 55

Gains from trade 50
  and international trade in securities 56
Global univalence 37

Heckscher–Ohlin, model under uncertainty 6–9
Heckscher–Ohlin Theorem 41
  and foreign ownership 43
  price version 46
  quantity version 42
  quantity version under uncertainty 44

International trade in securities and the gains from trade 56

INDEX

Labor, wages 7
Laspeyres
  price index 33
  quantity index 35, 36
Lerner symmetry, see tariffs
Lump sum transfers, and the gains from trade 51

Monopoly power
  in risk markets 83, 84
  in spot markets 79, 80, 81
  measurement of in risk markets, example 84

Nash-constrained Pareto optima 60

Pareto Inferior Trade, example 58
Portfolio 10
  choice problem 10–11, 17
  first order conditions 11
Prices
  normal price response under uncertainty 47
Production, see Firm
Profits, see Firm

Quotas 61
  equivalence with tariffs 71
  quota superior to a tariff 72, 73
  tariff superior to a quota 74

Real security 23
Risk
  degrees of risk sharing in markets 24, 25
  insurance function of markets 11, 12
  largeness or smallness in markets for 63
  prices for 11, 15
Risk aversion and ranking of tariffs and quotas 72, 73, 74, 75
Rybczynski Theorem 34
  failure under uncertainty if only spot prices fixed 35

  generalization to uncertainty in terms of spot and risk prices 35, 36

Security, choice of 10
Security valuation 13, 14
Spanning 13, 21, 22
  and factor price equalization 38
  and the Heckscher–Ohlin Theorem 44, 46
Spot markets 8, 9
  largeness or smallness in 63
Stockholder agreement about project value 16, 17, 21
Stolper–Samuelson Theorem 28
  definition of real rewards under uncertainty 29
  failure in terms of future spot prices 30–32
  validity in terms of price index 33
Symmetry of export and import taxes 67

Tariffs 61
  ad valorem 71, 72
  equivalence with quotas 71
  failure of Lerner symmetry 70
  optimal 80
  protective effect of 62, 63
  quota superior to a tariff 72, 73
  specific 71, 72
  state-specific 71, 72
  symmetry of export or import taxes 67, 68
  tariff superior to a quota 74

Uncertainty, state of nature 4
Univalence, global 37
Univalence, local 40, 41
Utility
  for portfolio choice 10
  change under uncertainty 78